Attitudes
for Fruitful
Christian
Living

PHYLLIS JEMMOTT

ISBN: 9798852623997

Independently Published in the United Kingdom
Editorial Production: The Editor's Chair
info@editorschair.com

ACKNOWLEDGEMENTS

I am deeply grateful to Almighty God for His unceasing favour and guidance throughout this remarkable journey. His hand has been evident in every step.

I extend my heartfelt thanks to Mr. and Mrs. Caroline-Lyn Val Anderson for their unwavering encouragement and support. Your belief in me has been a constant source of inspiration.

I would also like to express my appreciation to Destiny Media, particularly Geoff, for their continuous communication and assistance during the writing process. Your involvement has been invaluable.

A special acknowledgement goes to Pastor Richard Young for his genuine interest in my work and for being a significant part of my journey. Your wisdom and guidance have enriched this project.

I would be remiss not to mention Roselyn Creaser, whose unwavering encouragement during challenging times has kept me going. Your support has been a true blessing.

Lastly, I want to express my deep gratitude to Denise Roberts for her unwavering faith in me and for being a constant source of strength. Your belief in my abilities has been instrumental in the completion of this endeavour.

To all of you who have provided support, encouragement, and prayers throughout this undertaking, I offer my heartfelt thanks. Your presence in my life has made a significant difference, and I am forever grateful.

Thank you all,

Phyllis

PREFACE

The word 'attitude' is defined as the state of things or a person's state of mind, character, or behaviour, and can be either negative or positive. Thus, attitude ultimately describes an individual's feelings expressed through emotion and action. An individual can demonstrate their attitude through feelings such joy, laughter or sadness without speaking.

A person's attitude may be easily expressed through habits, lifestyle, and circumstances that can be noticed over time. It is extremely important not to judge individuals based solely on their outward manifestations. It is better to give allowances because we have no idea what the person may be going through or feeling internally. It could be a bad day or the wrong time, and interruptions can bring out unintended negative behaviour.

Negative behaviour can easily drive friends and colleagues away from your company. This can be evident among both the young and mature. For example, constant crying and moaning from small children can be pitiful and attention-seeking. Sadly, the same pattern of negative attitude can also exist among parents and leaders who desperately seek acknowledgement from others in their group. They do everything in their power to gain attention, such as speaking loudly, sulking, frowning, or waving their hand to draw attention.

Having the right attitude is often the most effective way to influence family, friends or colleagues. As members of the group, team or community, each person can support the other by refraining from wrong motives such as contentiousness, strife, selfishness, and unworthy ends. They should esteem the other by being concerned for the interests of others as well as their own interests. The opposite attitudes would be:

- Being insensitive and doing what you want regardless of who may be hurt by it.

- Being oversensitive and doing nothing for fear of displeasing someone.

- Being a 'yes' person by going along with everything to gain people's approval rather than seeking approval from God. In this age of 'me first' and looking out for oneself, making the good of others one of our primary goals will develop a serving attitude that pleases God.

As we get into our exploration of attitudes, let us recognise that cultivating a healthy attitude is akin to nourishing our bones, providing sustenance and enrichment that benefits us on multiple levels.

TABLE OF CONTENTS

INTRODUCTION

I am truly delighted to present this informative book that consists of various examples relating to people's attitudes towards one another. It demonstrates how God's word can serve as a solution for every negative attitude that exists among His children. However, it is important to note that while there may be solutions to attitude problems, this does not suggest some magical force that can instantly dispel negative behaviour among humans. We need to work at this if we are to live more fruitful and constructive lives.

The information presented in the book is derived from the teachings of the Bible and the experiences of individuals from various walks of life. It aims to help readers develop positive attitudes that will result in a more fruitful life. The aim of the book is to stimulate the minds of readers of every age, culture, and ethnicity. It is designed to be provocative.

The contents of the book highlight various aspects and examples of individual attitudes across everyday life and circumstances. It explores how an individual's behaviour can be motivated and changed through positive actions, without pretending to be what they are not. It offers positive suggestions that readers are free to take from the book and apply to improve their own attitudes. By doing so, they will experience the difference it will make to their lives.

This book is also suitable for every occasion where attitude matters, such as in work, family and social settings. It is helpful for building good relationship ethics among others in general. Every human expresses and possesses two types of attitude: positive and negative. A basic reason why people behave negatively towards others is possibly selfishness and jealousy. They often neglect to examine their own attitude, which can be infectious, overwhelming, and short-sighted. Therefore, a radical change is needed to understand the various aspects of these attitudes, which can affect others across genders and in communities, including church and social gatherings.

The sole purpose of this book is to draw your attention to the subject and comparisons of human attitudes. It examines the similarities that exist in society, such as in homes, schools, workplaces, organisations, and among all age groups, genders, and cultures. Although there may be instances where individuals from different backgrounds display negative attitudes, it is important to note that even our own attitudes can sometimes be wrong. On a personal note, the title of the book compelled me to evaluate my own behaviour and how I treat others. This self-reflection has been an eye-opener. The book plays a vital part in my everyday lifestyle, among my family, friends, associates, and in general, regardless of age or gender.

Adopting a new mindset has proven to be more effective in fostering meaningful relationships with others. Someone from another country may struggle to express themselves clearly in the local language, leading others to mistakingly believe that they are displaying a negative attitude, simply because the onlooker is unfamiliar with their cultural background. This can cause fear, suspicion and misinterpretation, but understanding can be achieved by attentively listening to the tone of their language and patiently allowing them to express themselves.

In the workplace, employers who display negative behaviour such as ignoring or talking over others, shouting, swearing, finger-pointing or hostility exert an overpowering attitude towards their staff. Similarly, some Christian leaders may also exhibit negative attitudes towards their congregations and other leaders, peers, or members of organisations. It is not uncommon for believers to encounter such negative expressions of attitudes, but conscience eventually speaks out.

Furthermore, there may be other disturbing negative attitudes evident among married couples and partners. For example, a husband and wife can unknowingly engage in a subtle power struggle against each other. Some wives may employ secretive tactics to project a negative attitude towards their husbands without uttering a word. In such instances, a challenging conflict may develop between the couple, with both parties unaware of the tactics being used to gain attention without verbal communication.

For instance, an ugly frown during times of love and play can convey messages like "don't touch" or "don't come too close". A husband may notice changes in his wife's behaviour, a lack of usual attention, while the wife may feel ignored and cold-shouldered by her husband. If such behaviour continues unchecked, the couple may lose focus, disrespect each other, and allow resentment to grow.

It is crucial to address and seek solutions for the deteriorating relationship between husband and wife. Ignoring the issue without seeking professional marriage counselling can lead to an escalation of problems and reflect carelessness on both sides. Negative behaviour should not be tolerated or allowed to dominate homes, schools, churches, communities, or workplaces. Unhealthy behaviours must be positively addressed and replaced with a right attitude. Negative behaviour, even without words, has the potential to drive others away, such as in the interactions between two people who were once friends but no longer talk to each other.

Genuine understanding and active listening are valuable skills in professional fields, especially when applied compassionately to help individuals change their attitudes towards one another. Demonstrating behavioural changes quietly can strengthen relationships unexpectedly. Therefore, individuals should never accept the idea of engaging in bad behaviour against another human being. Instead, they should seek ways to help others and foster positive attitudes that are more enduring.

Sometimes, individuals may exhibit negative behaviour while appearing sympathetic, often blaming the other person who may be suffering from other disorders or behavioural needs. On the other hand, individuals with a positive outlook can demonstrate the right attitude, which is more effective than other approaches.

One

Human Attitudes

The entire human race is inhabited by attitudes—some are good and some are bad. It may seem that you cannot get rid of your attitude as easily as you wish, but it should never be the case for not trying to learn how to develop a good attitude. It may seem hopeless when you endeavour to attain and maintain a good moral attitude, as you are presented with hindrances that block your mind from changing. It can seem easier to revert back to a bad attitude. This is especially so when a wrong attitude is at its worst among humans. When people who are already experiencing difficulties such as personal family crises, disasters, rejections, disappointments and bereavement experience negative behaviour from other people, it can impact them in extreme ways.

For example, navigating through the lockdown periods—a period of stress where you are not sure of what's coming—people were apt to behave with a wrong attitude due to various changes to what they were allowed or forbidden to do. When individuals are uncertain about the future, it can feel devastating and fearful. People become desperate, anxious and focused on survival. From time to time, older people may experience various hindering factors, and their behaviour can rapidly change due to changes in their appearance, the onset of disabilities, missing out on activities they once enjoyed, memory loss, loneliness, and fear of dying. These factors can often be the cause of negativity towards anyone, young or old, who crosses their path.

Therefore, you must understand that it is normal that different people struggle with different attitudes and behaviours. We may blame others without considering that they might be experiencing stress of their own—stress brought on by others, such as from children, work, money worries, health issues, and more. These factors can add to serious health issues; however, it should not be the case that we allow a deadly issue to develop simply because of an impure attitude. It is important to discern what should be processed and what should be avoided.

EXAMINE YOUR ATTITUDE

The entire world is full of people with similar attitudes. For a positive solution, everyone should take time to examine their own attitude. Imagine what a peaceful world it would be! Individuals who possess good morals and a positive attitude have likely developed these traits through years of parental guidance, education, and perhaps even divine intervention. These positive experiences can be nurtured within a strong foundation of discipline. This can be subtle, achieved and cultivated through a gentler approach to positive thinking. Having the right attitude is not only acceptable behaviour; it promotes health and longevity. That is why we should never make assumptons about why a person behaves the way they do. It is crucial that we show patience and understanding towards others because this is itself a healthy attitude. We need to understand that when a person displays a negative attitude, it may stem from factors such as lack of confidence, low self-esteem, or perhaps experiences of rejection and dismissal from others. Rather than pointing fingers at others, it is important to make an effort to understand the root causes of one's own negative attitude. In many cases, the majority of those fingers are pointing inward and back at us.

All humans are capable of expressing both negative and positive attitudes, even religious individuals and clergy members. They can struggle with major attitude problems. All human beings have attitudes, yet few are qualified or brave enough to confront and address them honestly. These are serious concerns that need desperate attention. We might ask ourselves, "What will it take to break free from this monster of a wrong attitude towards others?" It requires making a significant impact with words of encouragement, taking positive action, and possibly discovering the underlying causes of negative attitudes in individuals.

Although it may be extremely difficult to confront the truth about your own personal attitude, the proper way to deal with such a painful situation is to ask God for help in restoring a positive behaviour towards others. It can be concerning when individuals are unaware of their negative attitudes and the potential harm they can cause to others. For instance, when people treat others with contempt and unfairness without allowing them to understand the truth about their own attitudes, it becomes challenging to solve such behaviour from a distance.

A positive solution is necessary to address human behaviour: treating others as you would like to be treated. Sadly, this simple attitude can sometimes become a stumbling block and lead to the loss of friendships. Good friends are important, and it shouldn't be a big debate to speak the truth in love and mirror your own attitude in a positive way, especially if you're genuinely considering making changes for more realistic behaviour. There are instances of positive and unreasonable behaviour towards individuals with disabilities or mental impairments that may never be fully understood by those without firsthand experience. For example, a blind or disabled person may struggle to navigate crowded spaces as swiftly as others. It is important to put yourself in their shoes and consider how a sight-impaired person, for example, manages in the dark, relying solely on senses such as touch, scent and sound when they are unable to see.

Can you imagine the state of mind of a physically impaired individual who wakes up each day in the same position, relying on others to provide personal care? As caregivers, it is essential to develop a positive attitude towards those under your supervision, especially when they face challenging disorders and physical limitations. Even when no one is around, there is an unseen eye watching the way you perform your duties and how well you treat those who are unable to look after themselves. While admitting negative attitudes within oneself can be extremely difficult, it is worth doing the work. Why not ask a friend what they have observed about your character instead of doing nothing? Take a moment to reflect on your attitude towards others with mental and physical disabilities.

ACCEPT POSITIVE CRITICISM TO GROW

Not everyone will be in the right frame of mind to accept criticism, whether constructive or destructive, but making the choice to listen and accept the truth is the best option. It can greatly benefit a person to change their behaviour and accept others in the right way without altering the message of Jesus Christ, which is the truth. A transformation of truth is necessary to renew the mind from negative attitudes to positivity, enabling people to discover behaviour that is right towards others and God.

Perhaps when your understanding awakens, God will open your heart to much more than you could ever comprehend, leading you to discover the purpose for your life. If you seek the mercy of Jesus and become aware of the Father's heart, understanding His love for His creation, you cannot have an attitude of insecurity. He is God and knows all things. When dealing with individuals expressing poor attitudes towards others, it is worth your while to encourage them to adopt a change of attitude. It is not a life sentence. Precious truth spoken in love, served with a little ointment of gentleness and patience to soothe the pain, can make a difference. I have experienced the impact of this mixture many times, and it has done me good.

It is important to be aware of how people are quick to point out the faults and failures of others without realising their own shortcomings. Rather than saying, "I'm not like that" and trying to avoid fixing the problem, you can approach life's challenges with a more compassionate and understanding attitude. The above words encompass it all. There is no definitive solution, but hopefully, you will discover a new understanding of attitude and why people behave the way they do. Since the beginning of creation, humans have inherited an innate and unreasonable behaviour that exists throughout the world. Therefore, perceptions of individual attitudes come from various cultures, particularly among young individuals from countries experiencing devastating persecution. How can you contribute to making their lives more livable? Will you sidestep and treat them with contempt, or will you recognise their need for assistance and offer a friendly smile that says, "I see where I can change my selfish attitude towards you" and smile more genuinely?

Christian Attitudes Towards Christ

W ho is Christ? Christ is the Son of God and the Anointed One. The title "Christ" is also used when referring to the Christian congregation and its relationship to the Lord Jesus Christ.

The Word (Christ), who became flesh and lived among men, revealed His glory to us as the only begotten Son who receives fullness from His Father, abounding in grace and truth. The Christian attitude towards Christ involves acknowledging Him as the uniquely begotten Son of God. Christ is the Lord of your personal life, and establishing a relationship with Him entails adopting a similar attitude to that of Christ Jesus. *"Who, being in very nature God, did not consider equality with God something to be used to his own advantage; rather, he made himself nothing by taking the very nature of a servant, being made in human likeness."* (Philippians 2:6-7)

In foretelling His birth, the angel instructed Joseph to name the child Mary was carrying Jesus. The personal name of Jesus, combined with the title Christ, draws attention to the person Himself—the One who was eventually revealed as the Anointed One of God. This occurred when Jesus turned thirty years of age and was baptised in water, and was confirmed when a dove descended upon Him (see John 1:32). The title "Christ" is often used alone, but it is also expressed as "Jesus Christ", which is equivalent to the Hebrew term "Messiah". Christ or Messiah is the One anointed by God with His Spirit to be the universal King. This was foretold centuries before Jesus' birth; however, at the time of His birth, Jesus was not yet revealed to the world as the Anointed One or Christ.

Christ signifies a unique relationship that distinguishes His Sonship from that of His disciples. No one else is called the "*Word that dwelt among men*". John says of Him, "*we beheld His glory, the glory of the only begotten of the Father, full of grace and truth*" (John 1:14 KJV). This title describes a relationship of equality, as the Son of God is no less than God Himself. Jesus claimed to be one with the Father, speaking of a unity of substance with the Father, indicating equality in all the attributes of deity. Jesus said, "*I and the Father are one.*" (John 10:30)

The title "Christ" also emphasises Christ's role as one of the greatest revelations of God. Christ alone possesses knowledge of the Father and serves as the sole mediator of this knowledge. Jesus said, "*I am the way and the truth and the life; no one comes to the Father except through me*" (see John 14:6). This is why the Jews sought to stone Him for professing Himself equal with God.

At the time of Jesus' birth, shepherds near Bethlehem, caring for their sheep, received an angelic announcement foreseeing Jesus' future role. They were told, *"For this day in the city of David there has been born for you a Savior, who is Christ the Lord (the Messiah)"* (Luke 2:11, AMP).

Some may refer to the eternal generation, signifying its timelessness. The glory of the Word made flesh was such that it befitted the only begotten Son of God and could not belong to anyone else. Jesus Christ is the only begotten of the Father, and believers are children of God by His special favour of adoption, having the image of His perfection through the special graces of regeneration.

Jesus Christ, as a man, did not give up His deity to become human, but rather set aside His glory and power in submission to His Father's will. Although Christ limited His power and knowledge, He was not subjected to the constraints of place, time, and other human limitations. Christ's humanity represents freedom from sin, which helps us recognise the Spirit of God.

THE EXPRESSION OF GOD

Not only did Jesus say that He is equal to God but also the exact representation of God, not just reflecting God's image but revealing God Himself. Jesus imitates the nature of God, being both spiritual and bodily, though the Father is invisible to human eyes. *"Therefore God exalted him to the highest place and gave him the name that is above every name, that at the name of Jesus every knee should bow, in heaven and on earth and under the earth and every tongue acknowledge that Jesus Christ is Lord, to the glory of God the Father"* (Philippians 2:9-11).

Christ has always existed with God and is equal to God because He is God. However, Christ, being God, became a man in order to fulfill God's plan of salvation. He did not merely appear as a man, but actually became human to identify with our sins. Out of love for the Father, He voluntarily laid aside His divine rights and privileges. Christ died on the cross for our sins so that we would not face eternal death. God glorified Jesus because of His obedience and raised Him to His original position at the Father's right hand, where He will reign forever as our Lord and Judge. As Christians, we should be obedient to Christ. The Spirit acknowledges that Jesus Christ came in the flesh from God. So *"every spirit that does not confess that Jesus Christ has come in the flesh is not of God. And this is the spirit of the Antichrist, which you have heard was coming, and is now already in the world."* (1 John 4:3 NKJV)

One day, Jesus came from Galilee to the Jordan to be baptised by John. Though John protested strenuously to prevent Him from being baptised, saying, *"'I need to be baptized by You, and are You coming to me?' But Jesus answered and said to him, 'Permit it to be so now, for thus it is fitting for us to fulfill all righteousness.' Then he allowed Him."* (Matthew 15:14-15 NIV)

John took a positive attitude to fulfill what Christ intended to show the world by allowing Himself to be subjected and baptised by a mere man like himself. God is all-powerful, the Creator of the world, and knows about the empires of the earth long before they come into being. Pride and power cause nations to rebel against God and try to break free from Him.

The world has many leaders boasting of their power, ranting and raving against God and His people, and promising to take over, forming their own empires. However, God laughs because all power they have comes from Him and can be taken away at any time. Thus, people may eventually wonder in what sense God is the Father of Christ, and Christ the Son of God. The answer to this question is not a simple one. However, you need to understand that the title "Son of God" does not speak of a physical nature like that of a man.

God is a spirit, and Christ, the Son of God, assumed a human body in Bethlehem. Thus, He is shown to be of a different league to the angels. God declares, *"YOU ARE MY SON, TODAY I HAVE BEGOTTEN (fathered) YOU [declared Your authority and rule over the nations]"* (Hebrews 1:5 AMP). The narrowness of God's way should be a sober incentive to take the message to the entire world. He has come to impart to every person the life of the Father, and the way to Christ's kingdom is through the new birth. This miracle of the Spirit, performed by the Holy Spirit, is not based on blood or the will of the flesh. All who welcome Jesus Christ as Lord into their lives are reborn spiritually and receive His new life from God through faith.

THE NEW BIRTH

The new birth changes individuals from the inside out, rearranging their attitudes, desires, and motives. Being born of the flesh makes them physically alive and places them in the family of their earthly parents. Being born of God makes them spiritually alive and puts them in the family of God. To those who believe in and rely on His name, God gives them the authority and privilege to become His children (see John 1:12). Christians are born again as new creations; the old person is gone, and the new has come. When a person repents, confesses their sins to God, and receives forgiveness, and believes in their heart and confesses with their mouth that Jesus Christ is Lord, their attitude towards Christ changes. There is a process from negative behaviour to a positive attitude. One must repent of all known sins, confess Jesus Christ as Lord, and be willing to come to God on His terms. A Christian attitude and confession of faith involve demonstrating works from the heart, believing that Jesus died and rose again from the dead, and confessing with the mouth.

Therefore, to become a Christian, one must be born again into the family of God through Jesus Christ and have the Spirit of God living in them. John warns believers not to believe every spirit but to discern whether they come from God. Again, he gave us a simple way to do so, which is to check whether a spirit acknowledges and confesses that Jesus Christ came in the flesh and has God as His source (see 1 John 4:2). It is declared to Christian believers, *"Now you are Christ's body and individually members of it"* (see 1 Corinthians 12:27) in a spiritual sense. Those who were baptised into Christ's death have the hope of being joint heirs with Christ in the heavenly kingdom.

There are many ways to test teachers to see if their message is truly from the Lord. You should check if their words align with what God says in the Bible. Other tests can include their commitment to the body of believers, their lifestyle, and the fruit of their ministry. However, the most important test is believing that Christ Jesus is the visible, tangible image of the invisible God. He is the reality of all God's promises and the complete revelation of who God is. As Jesus explained when Philip asked to see the Father, *"Anyone who has seen me has seen the Father"*

(John 14:19 NKJV). To know Jesus is to know God. Thus, the search for truth and reality ends in Christ

Human limitations means our ordinary abilities cannot serve as a means to recognise the Spirit of God. The Spirit acknowledges that Jesus Christ has come in the flesh from God, and places this revelation into the spirit of man. In Matthew 16:14-17, Jesus asks His disciples, *"who do men say I am?"* to which the disciples repeated what others had been saying about Him. Jesus then asks, *"But who do you say I am?"* Peter then replies, *"You are the Christ, the Son of the living God"* (NKJV). Upon hearing this, Jesus tells Peter that he did not come to this knowledge through *"flesh and blood"*, meaning Peter did not source that knowledge through his own spirit. Jesus, as the only unique Son or the only begotten of God, is in the intimate presence of the Father, declaring and revealing Him to all. He has made the Father known (see John 1:18).

As the firstborn over all creation, Christ holds the priority and authority of a firstborn prince in a king's household. The firstborn man was made from the dust, but the second man, referring to Christ, is the Lord from heaven and not of the dust of the earth. Christ, being the life-giving agent, entered into a new form of existence through His resurrection. He is the source of spiritual life, and through Him, believers will experience resurrection and receive transformed, eternal bodies suited to their new eternal life (see Philippians 3:21).

Therefore, Christ is completely holy and the Lord of all. He possesses the authority to judge the world and all of creation, including the spirit world. Jesus Christ demonstrated humility and willingly gave up His rights so that He could obey God and serve people. His example teaches us to have a servant attitude, serving others out of love for God and genuine care, not out of guilt. As believers, we can choose to approach life with the right attitude, having positive expectations and looking for opportunities to serve others, showing genuine interest and taking positive actions to maintain unity among believers. God, as the Creator and sustainer of the world, holds everything together, protects it from disintegration and chaos, and sustains life. Therefore, no one is independent of Him; all are His servants. *"For in him all things were created: things in heaven and on earth, visible and invisible, whether thrones or powers or rulers or authorities; all things have been created through him and for him. He is before all things, and in him all things hold together"* (Colossians 1:16-17).

A KINGDOM NOT OF THIS WORLD

The disciples initially believed that Jesus would establish an earthly kingdom to free Israel from Roman oppression. James and John, along with their mother, desired honoured positions in Christ's kingdom. However, Jesus revealed that His kingdom was not centred on physical places and thrones, but on the transformation of the heart and lives of His followers. Though the disciples could not fully comprehend this concept until after Jesus' resurrection, He did not ridicule them for asking or deny their request. You are free to ask Jesus for what you need or want, but He will give what is best, even if it means denying certain requests for your own good.

At the time when James and John requested the highest positions in Jesus' kingdom, He taught them that true greatness comes from serving others. While the world often measures greatness by personal achievements, in Christ's kingdom, serving others is the path to greatness. The desire to be on top will only hinder and not help. Instead, you should seek ways to minister to the needs of others, foster unity among fellow workers, and make positive changes. Your thoughts and actions should be motivated by love, holding them in subjection. In contrast to those who exercise authority and dominion, Jesus warns, *"But this is not how it is among you; instead, whoever wishes to become great among you must be your servant, and whoever wishes to be first* and *most important among you must be slave of all"* (see Mark 10:43-44 AMP).

Three

Attitudes Towards Conversion

A person who has been recently converted should not be nominated for a leadership position, as they may become self-centred and fall into the same judgment as the devil. Instead, they should be given time to develop a good reputation and demonstrate the right attitude. It is important that new members of the church become secure and strong in their faith before being inducted into leadership positions. This is especially crucial when the church is seeking workers to fill vacancies in departments, as hasty decisions to place new believers in senior positions, without proper training and understanding of the role, can lead to failure and potential disgrace.

Spiritual growth through Bible study and prayer is essential before new believers can take on leadership roles. While they can serve in various capacities, it is important for them to be firmly grounded in the faith before assuming leadership responsibilities. This also applies to volunteers who aspire to become leaders in the body of Christ. They should be guided and first learn how to serve at home before serving in the church. Without proper training, they may become discouraged when inevitable challenges arise. As it is said, if a man is not willing to care for, disciple, and teach his children, he is not qualified to lead the church (see I Timonty 3:1-7). Thankfully, many churches have learned valuable lessons from hasty leader appointments and have made efforts to correct these practices.

When it is time to appoint a leader, age or gender should never be a problem. Wisdom, discipline, and maturity are the most important prerequisites for Christian service. Every born-again believer should seek to share their story of how they were saved, practicing a form of evangelism that begins at home, within the church, and extends to the outer world. This should be encouraged. However, there are additional conditions that must be met. Believers should not hold grudges against anyone or pray with selfish motives. Their prayer requests should be focused on the good of God's kingdom and not motivated by personal interests and desires. It is important to think of others and be willing to share with them what God has done, knowing that He can do the same or even more for others. It is a joyful experience to see one's prayers answered. Therefore, when praying, it is important to not only express personal desires to God but also to ask for His will to be done in one's life.

Having the right attitude during an individual's conversion means leading them to understand their immediate condition and the need for repentance. Repentance involves admitting one's honest need for a saviour, with Jesus being available to fulfill that role. It also entails dedicating one's life to God's holy worshipping service, putting off old ways and embracing Christ. It is important to change one's attitude and repent; otherwise, one may perish. Salvation is not achieved by simply turning over a new leaf or attempting to reform oneself. It is achieved through faith in Christ that turns scarlet sins as white as snow (see Isaiah 1:18). Scripture tells us that the righteousness of a man would be like filthy rags had it not been for the righteousness of Christ (see Isaiah 64:6 and Romans 5:19). The redemption of man comes through God's free grace, His unmerited favour, and is received by faith that leads to confession and transformation. It is not the result of striving or personal effort; it is a gift from God. Responding to this gift with gratitude, praise, and joy is crucial. As Ephesians 2:8 says, *"For it is by grace you have been saved, through faith—and this is not from yourselves, it is the gift of God."*

If someone has sincerely trusted God for their salvation and acknowledged the Lord, the Holy Spirit will enter their heart and bring about the necessary changes from the inside out, gradually transforming their behaviour, desires, and thoughts. This change is a process and does not happen overnight. The transformation is evident in one's outward expression, and others will notice the change. Being born again is not about physically reentering one's mother's womb but rather experiencing the transformation brought about by the precious blood of Jesus Christ.

If one has already repented and expressed godly sorrow for their past sins, there is no need to dwell on them further. God's forgiveness is complete, and He remembers our sins no more. The focus should shift towards living a life that pleases God and aligns with His Word. This involves growing in faith, seeking to know God more intimately, and allowing His Spirit to guide and empower us.

God's character in the work of redemption is absolutely clear and glorious. His choice is to bring many sons to glory, adopting and regenerating them as sons of God. Before anyone can enter His heavenly glory, they must become sons of God. Christ, as the captain of salvation, has made this choice and seeks to find and perfect individuals through His work of redemption, shedding His blood to pave the way to the crown. Believers are united with Christ in this work of near union, with Him as the sanctifying agent. Christians now share the same human nature and have one spirit, the same mind as Christ, forming an endearing relation as brethren. So, how can a person become a Christian? Follow the guidelines outlined below.

CONFESSING CHRIST

What is your attitude when confessing Christ? We are told that those who are not ashamed of Christ will not be ashamed by Him, while those who reject Him bring reproach upon themselves. Individuals must confess Christ with their mouths and believe in their hearts that God raised Christ from the dead. Believers have a duty to encourage people everywhere with this vital message of how to receive Christ into their lives. By doing so, we can help these people obtain salvation. The gospel of salvation acknowledges that Christ is the anointed Saviour to the utmost, and confessing Jesus as the Lord of one's life is the fundamental step in this brave journey (see Romans 10:9).

Confessing the Lordship of Christ requires the assent of the will. It acknowledges that at the name of Jesus, every knee shall bow and every tongue confess that Jesus Christ is Lord (see Philippians 2:10-11). While some may view Christ as merely a man, He is much more than that. He is the Son of God, possessing the divine nature. It is perilous to deny the power, ability, and authority of God, especially for those who have no knowledge or awareness of Him. After all, the Father has exalted Jesus to a place of honour, giving Him a name above all names. Now that you have confessed Christ, it's time to receive Him.

RECEIVING CHRIST WITH THE RIGHT ATTITUDE

Individuals receive Christ with the help of the Holy Spirit, recognising their need for a saviour. Scripture said, *"As many as receive Him, to them He will give the right to become children of God, even to those who believe in His name"* (NKJV). By welcoming Jesus Christ as the Lord of their lives, individuals are reborn spiritually and receive new life from God through faith in Christ. This new birth transforms individuals from within, rearranging their attitudes, desires, and motives. It makes them spiritually alive and places them in the family of God. This fresh start is available to all who believe in Christ.

OBEDIENCE TO CHRIST

Jesus exemplified obedience by suffering and dying for the world, pleasing His Father. His perfect obedience demonstrated God's completeness, maturity, and the experience of suffering. Because of this, Jesus can empathise with human suffering and weaknesses during trials and distress. Sincere obedience in the Christian life comes from the heart, wholeheartedly obeying and fully giving oneself to God. It involves loving God with all one's heart, soul, and mind. True obedience involves submitting to God's authority, which in turn fosters positive relationships with God and others. This obedience can greatly improve family dynamics, leadership dynamics, and the overall dynamics within a church.

Every person has a master, either righteousness or sin. A Christian is not a person with sins but someone who is born again, washed and cleansed by the blood of Jesus, and has received newness of life. Christians belong to God and should develop the right attitude towards Him and others by listening and obeying with a willing heart. Jesus tells His disciples that if they love Him, they will obey His commandments and teachings. When disciples truly love Christ, they show it through their obedience. Love is a crucial aspect of obedience in the Christian character, extending beyond mere words to commitment and conduct. Therefore, if you love Christ, prove it by obeying His words.

Understanding Jesus' command to love others, true disciples seek to know the heart of the Father. God wants His children to love others, which is not a new commandment but a revolutionary concept. Loving others based on Jesus' sacrificial love requires believers to be strong and united in a world hostile to God. Jesus was a living example of God's love, and as His disciples, we are encouraged to be living examples of Jesus' life. Our Christian love should prove that we are His disciples. Divisions, jealousy, and bickering in worship are contrary to this attitude and reflect poorly on the disciples of Jesus.

During His earthly ministry, Jesus demonstrated many examples of obedience, setting positive standards for His followers to follow. He humbly offered prayers and petitions with loud cries and tears to the Father, who could have saved Him from death. His reverent submission to the Father made His prayers effective. Jesus' obedience to His Father, even in the face of great trials, serves as an inspiration for believers to be obedient, regardless of the cost.

Although Christ was the Son of God, He learned obedience through suffering and was made perfect. He became the source of eternal salvation for all who obey Him. Jesus' life was not a scripted play; rather, He freely chose to make the will of God the Father His own. By His example, Jesus made the choice to be obedient, knowing it would bring suffering and death.

LACK OF OBEDIENCE: A LESSON FROM KING SAUL

'To obey is better than sacrifice'.

King Saul's lack of obedience serves as a prime example of the consequences that can result from disregarding God's instructions. It is through his life that we learn the lesson, "to obey is better than sacrifice" (1 Samuel 15:22), and that lack of obedience can ultimately lead to rejection. Obedience holds great significance in the life of a follower of Christ so Saul's actions can teach us much.

King Saul received clear instructions from God to completely destroy Israel's enemies. However, Saul chose to save the best of the spoil and intended to offer it as a sacrifice to God. When the prophet Samuel confronted him, he asked Saul if the Lord delighted in burnt offerings and sacrifices more than obedience. He emphasised that a sacrifice is a ritual transaction between God and humanity, physically demonstrated to signify the relationship between them. In so doing, Samuel emphasised that obedience to the Lord is far more valuable than sacrifices or external rituals.

Saul's disobedience revealed a rebellious and arrogant attitude. He prioritised his own interests and the opinions of others over his relationship with God. His sacrifices became hollow and empty because his heart was not truly repentant and devoted to God. Consequently, God rejected Saul and took away his kingdom. Saul's rebellion against God was a grave sin that closed the door to forgiveness and restoration.

GOD'S EXPECTATION OF OBEDIENCE

Throughout the history of Israel, the people's disobedience and rebellion against God led to challenging periods. Although their behaviour deserved judgment, God showed them mercy, which can be defined as not receiving the punishment they deserved. Despite this mercy, the Israelites went through cycles of disobedience and forgetting God's instructions. The temptation to deviate from God's ways is ever-present, but we must remain determined and loyal to God, even amidst difficulties. It is crucial to establish a genuine purpose in life and remember that disobedience will lead to retribution and punishment. The Bible warns of everlasting destruction for those who do not know and obey the gospel, resulting in eternal separation from God.

God's disapproval towards sinful people who replace the truth about Him with their own fantasies is understandable. He does not suppress the truth to accommodate their lifestyles, as His nature is morally perfect. God expects obedience from the heart, surpassing mere religious rituals, relationship, activity, achievement, or possession. True obedience requires complete submission of our will, even if it means breaking our stubbornness. It involves committing our minds and hearts to seeking God, His principles, and His values. Recognising that our bodies are temples of God, we should use our strength, talents, and sexuality for His pleasure and fulfillment according to His guidelines.

Lasting obedience can only be achieved through a positive relationship with God. Mankind lacks the ability to remain obedient without the enablement of the Holy Spirit. While some may initially strive to obey God by their own strength and good intentions, they often fail miserably. No amount of law-keeping, self-improvement, or religious discipline can make one right with God without the empowering presence of the Holy Spirit. Maintaining the right attitude will help develop a strong foundation and a positive mindset, enabling us to provide support and solve problems for those facing challenges. A positive attitude greatly improves communication, support, and problem-solving, ultimately allowing us to follow Christ confidently.

FOLLOWING JESUS

Jesus provides clear instructions to His followers, emphasising the need to deny oneself, lose sight of personal interests, take up the cross, and follow Him. These requirements are stated upfront, not in the middle or along the journey. Jesus expects true discipleship to be accompanied by action and unwavering loyalty, without neglecting family responsibilities (see Matthew 16:24).

As followers of Christ, we must take an interest in His teachings, actions, and interactions with people from diverse backgrounds. Jesus teaches us excellent qualities for relating to people of all races, religions, and ethnicities. By developing an obedient attitude and deepening our knowledge of Christ, we can become faithful followers and encourage others to do the same.

When Jesus called Peter and Andrew to follow Him, they immediately left their fishing nets and followed without considering the cost. Their willingness and quick response allowed them to become faithful followers and help others find God. Jesus called these men away from their productive trade of fishing to become spiritually productive. Following Jesus requires discipline, commitment, and a willingness to forsake one's former life. Jesus used the metaphor of carrying one's cross to illustrate the seriousness of this commitment. The disciples understood that taking up their crosses meant being willing to risk even death while fishing for souls in the kingdom of God. They were aware that following Jesus might lead to the loss of their lives, but they were prepared to pay the price.

Jesus is still calling men away from selfish pursuits and into the kingdom. For some people that could entail leaving your employment. One example is when Jesus called Matthew, the tax collector, to follow Him. It required courage for Jesus to choose him as one of His inner circle of disciples, considering that tax collectors were often social outcasts and classified with sinners due to the abuses associated with their job. As a tax collector, Matthew was likely literate and accustomed to note-taking as part of his business activities. When Jesus called Matthew, he rose up and left everything behind, except his pen. He nobly used his literary skills to become the first person to compile an account of the teachings of Jesus, forsaking his job to follow Him. Matthew, an excellent writer, is an example of someone who gave up his accounting job to become one of Christ's followers.

Jesus came to call sinners to repentance, not the righteous. You need to imitate Jesus in reality. You cannot save your physical life from death, pain, or discomfort. By turning your life inward, you will lose your intended purpose. In other words, when you give your life in service to Christ, you will discover the true purpose of living—following Him, allowing the Word of God to take deep root in your heart, and being motivated to live a positive life of change.

IMMITATE

Followers of Christ should imitate Christ's teachings, what He says, and copy His attitude towards people, even those who hated Him. He expects total dedication from His followers, not half-hearted commitment or selective adherence to His ideas. This means accepting the cross along with the crown, judgment as well as mercy, and being willing to sacrifice friendships, leisure time, treasures, habits, and anything that may hinder total commitment to living for Him. During Jesus' earthly ministry, a man came desiring to follow Him, but he wanted to first go and bury his father. Perhaps this man wanted to delay following Jesus and use his father's burial as an excuse. Jesus replied, *"Let the dead bury their own dead"* (see Matthew 8:21-22).

Christ demands true commitment, even to the point of risking death and not turning back. Real discipleship implies real commitment, pledging one's whole existence to the service of God. While some people prefer to follow Jesus as they please, never finding the time to humble themselves and pray, a time is coming when every knee shall bow. No matter where you may travel, you must follow the Lord, keeping your eyes on Him and trusting in His holy word. Determine not to leave Him, hold His hand, and let Him guide you to that promised land. Just as a soldier follows his captain and a slave follows his master, believers should follow Christ as their commander and Lord. By following Christ, no one will lose their way (see John 6:39 and Matthew 4:19). Following Jesus requires self-sacrifice, and each individual must be ready to follow Him. It requires self-denial and taking up the cross daily.

You may ask, "What does Jesus want from me?" The proper attitude of a follower is to imitate what Christ did, not just talking the talk but walking the walk. It means expressing genuine love for the Father and responding to the needs of others, just as Jesus did. People in general are inclined to imitate the attitude and behaviour of others, especially if it looks good and seems easy to adapt. Just as friends imitate each other in the hope of acceptance, people often imitate bad company instead of seeking to imitate good examples. However, true followers of Christ are encouraged to *"Follow God's example, therefore, as dearly loved children and walk in the way of love, just as Christ loved us and gave himself up for us as a fragrant offering and sacrifice to God"* (Ephesians 5:1-2). Children are the best imitators of good parenting, imitating positive behaviours they observe in their parents. They desire to grow up and become like their parents. Similarly, believers should imitate Christ in love and affection, going beyond self-sacrificing service. However, many people are unwilling to imitate Christ in His suffering. While suffering can vary in length and severity, Jesus taught that His followers should be prepared to endure persecution and remain faithful. They were called disciples because they were willing to patiently endure suffering. True followers of Christ are those who are willing to endure suffering for His sake, even though some suffering may be self-inflicted due to living in a fallen world. They should also consider the suffering of Christ, who never sinned but suffered to set men free from the domain of sin.

The cost of following Christ must be carefully considered, and any conditions that might become hindrances should be set aside. Jesus commanded complete loyalty and obedience, which should take priority over one's own desires and challenge personal priorities. The journey of following Christ can be likened to wayward sheep going astray. The Good Shepherd, Jesus, seeks after those lost sheep and calls them to return to the fold. As followers of Christ, we are called to imitate His example and follow His lead, even when it means forsaking our own desires and priorities.

To imitate Christ means to embody His teachings and emulate His character. It means loving others unconditionally, just as He loved us. Jesus showed compassion to the poor, the outcast, and the marginalised. He healed the sick, fed the hungry, and ministered to those in need. As His followers, we are called to do likewise, extending love and kindness to all people, regardless of their circumstances or social standing.

Imitating Christ also means living a life of humility and service. Jesus, the King of Kings, humbled Himself and washed the feet of His disciples. He taught us that true greatness lies in serving others. As His followers, we should adopt a servant's heart, seeking opportunities to serve and bless those around us.

Furthermore, imitating Christ involves embracing the way of the cross. Jesus willingly laid down His life for us, bearing our sins and offering redemption through His sacrifice. As His followers, we are called to take up our own crosses daily, dying to ourselves and living for Him. This may involve sacrificing our own ambitions, comforts, and worldly pursuits for the sake of the Kingdom.

Imitating Christ also means imitating His relationship with the Father. Jesus had an intimate and obedient relationship with God, constantly seeking His will and relying on His strength. As followers of Christ, we are called to cultivate a deep and personal relationship with God through prayer, studying His Word, and walking in obedience to His commands.

Ultimately, imitating Christ requires wholehearted commitment and surrender. It means aligning our will with His and allowing His Holy Spirit to transform us from the inside out. It is a lifelong journey of becoming more like Him, growing in faith, and conforming to His image.

EMBRACING A POSITIVE ATTITUDE TOWARDS GOD

Believers must not become sluggish in their attitude, but rather imitate Christ through faith and patience. When facing great challenges, it's easy to lose sight of the goal and think that God has forgotten you. However, it's important to know that God is never unjust or forgetful of your faithfulness in His service. Even in hard times when you feel low or left behind, and when you're not receiving immediate rewards or acclaim, take courage and continue without complaining. Your faithfulness will be rewarded.

God is aware of your sincere commitment to His service, and His promises are trustworthy and unchangeable. These two attributes are part of God's nature, as He embodies all truth. Be careful not to imitate evil, as all that is good comes from God. Those who do evil do not truly know or understand God (see 3 John 11).

No individual has the right to consider themselves better than others. In the sight of God, everyone stands on an equal level and needs someone who knows the way. Jesus calls everyone to imitate Him and learn from Him, assuring that those who trust in Him will not be lost. It is an excellent action to reflect on your attitude towards yourself and others, considering and ensuring that you are on the right path.

This positive action will also influence others to do the same. Jesus' teachings reveal a code of ethics and a standard of conduct for all believers. Reflect on the contrast between kingdom values and worldly values. In the kingdom of heaven, wealth, power, and authority are not important. Kingdom people should seek after things that pertain to the kingdom, such as peace, joy, and love for God and others. Cultivate positive attitudes that align with the blessings and benefits of the kingdom.

Ask yourself: Does your attitude reflect the selfishness, pride, and lust for power found in the world, or does it mirror the humility and self-sacrifice of Jesus, your King? Believers should meditate on the words of Christ and develop a positive relationship with Him that is unshakable. They should be able to see the difference between Christians and non-Christians. New followers of Jesus are not expected to instantly mature overnight; growth in Christ is a lifelong process. Be warned, however, for even though you have received a new nature and attitude through the Holy Spirit, your growth in Christ is not automatic. It requires patience and time to grow in grace and knowledge of the Lord Jesus. Christian growth requires daily step-by-step progress.

Some individuals believe that they can hide from God's sight, but they are mistaken. God's eyes search throughout the earth, beholding both good and evil. Humans usually serve something or somebody, whether it's an organisation or their own selfish desires. Just as a fish is not free when it leaves the water and a tree is not free when it leaves the soil, you are not free when you leave the Lord. True freedom is found in wholeheartedly serving the Lord.

Your life should be like seasoning that adds taste and flavour to the world. However, if your attitude lacks value and taste, like a Christian who makes no effort to positively impact the world, you will be of little value to God. If you love the things of the world more than loving God, it's no wonder that you are of no use to Him. Christians should not choose to blend in with everyone else but should strive to be effective witnesses with a positive attitude.

You cannot hide a light that is placed on top of a hill; it will shine brightly for miles. Your salvation is not based on deeds of service alone but on faith in Christ. However, if your faith lacks sincerity, it will not reach out to others. Enhancing your Christian attitude through spending quality time in fasting, prayer, and sacrificial acts will prove beneficial spiritually and physically. However, fasting, for example, helps only the person who engages in it. God desires your service to extend far beyond your own personal growth to acts of kindness, charity, justice, and generosity. True fasting is not just about what you refrain from consuming; it is about pleasing God by applying His word to society.

Living a Christ-centred lifestyle will cause your life to shine like a light, revealing who Christ is. On the contrary, hiding your light, remaining quiet when the opportunity arises to speak for Christ, or aligning with the wrong crowds and denying your identity, will cause your light to dim. Negative behaviour can hinder and hide the truth, diminishing your impact on the world. Instead of being a coward, find your real purpose and live according to positive Christian morals.

Reflect on the biblical example where a man sees the speck in his neighbour's eye but overlooks the log in his own (Matthew 7:3-5). Examine yourself through God's mirror, His Word, and ask the Holy Spirit to help you correct and rebuild your relationship with God. There is no better way to check your attitude than by using God's mirror. It will provide correction, direction, and guidance, always giving a true reading. When you significantly change your negative attitude and continue trusting God, making firm decisions to submit to His ways, you will experience relief and take the pressure off yourself.

Having faith helps solve problems, and you must continue to hold on and believe that God is faithful. He will deliver you in His own time, leading you to greener pastures. Your faith will gradually increase and help you in every situation. Instead of worrying and allowing negative thoughts and uneasiness to prevail, make the positive decision to rise up, give God praise, and meditate on His word. This will drive away every bad attitude of worry and bring it under subjection in the name of Jesus.

Just as Israel was tasked with being a witness by telling others about God and what He had done, believers in Christ have a duty to share the responsibility of being God's witnesses. Do people know what God is like through your words and example? Although humans cannot see God directly, they should see His reflection in and around you. God is holy and cannot ignore, excuse, or tolerate sin as if it doesn't matter. Most importantly, you need to understand that your sin will cut you off from God and act as a wall that isolates you from Him.

The Old Testament contains a long list of sinful behaviours that made God angry and forced Him to turn away. Those who lived in a life of sin and did not repent separated themselves from God forever. God could not accept them into His holy presence unless their sins were removed, and they heeded the warnings of deadly destruction if they remained in their sins.

Your attitude towards God should express a positive belief. It is not up for debate or questioning. Having a negative attitude towards the Supreme Almighty God, who is not a mere man and cannot be treated as such, is not appropriate. As individuals, we should look up to God in faith, as the giver of *"the substance of things hoped for, the evidence of things not seen"* (Hebrews 11:1 NKJV). Although we cannot physically see God, our faith allows us to look into His presence, which serves as evidence. Therefore, it is imperative to develop a positive attitude towards God. This reflection in the light of the Holy Scriptures helps us understand the need for one another and the importance of mutual love, mutual commerce, and the same light. We should possess a positive attitude towards God, even though we cannot see Him.

HOW ATTITUDE GROWS

For example, let's consider a couple who had two sons, Allan and Jerry, with different attitudes. The boys were taught the importance of giving an offering to the Lord at a certain time of the year, and it was up to them to decide what to give. When the time came, Allan, the older son, approached his parents with a negative attitude. He complained about having to give up his hard-earned money and grumbled about the inconvenience it caused him. He questioned why he had to give anything at all and argued that it was unnecessary.

On the other hand, Jerry, the younger son, displayed a positive attitude. He saw the opportunity to give as a chance to honour God and demonstrate his gratitude for all the blessings he had received. He cheerfully selected a portion of his earnings and joyfully offered it as his gift to God.

As time passed, Allan continued to harbour a negative attitude towards giving and other aspects of his faith. He became self-centred and focused only on his own desires and ambitions. His negative attitude hindered his spiritual growth, and he drifted away from God.

In contrast, Jerry's positive attitude towards God and his willingness to give extended beyond that one instance. He developed a habit of generosity and a heart that sought to serve others. His positive attitude opened doors for him to bless those in need and share the love of Christ with others. His relationship with God grew stronger, and he experienced joy, peace, and fulfillment in his life.

This simple story illustrates the importance of having a positive attitude towards God and the impact it can have on our relationship with Him. A negative attitude closes our hearts to His guidance and blessings, while a positive attitude opens us up to His transformative power and allows us to align our lives with His will.

Ultimately, cultivating a positive attitude towards God requires humility, trust, and a willingness to surrender our own desires and agendas. It involves seeking His presence, studying His Word, and allowing His Spirit to shape our thoughts and actions. When we approach God with a positive attitude, we position ourselves to receive His abundant grace, guidance, and blessings in our lives.

ATTITUDE BETWEEN LAWYERS AND CLIENTS

The relationship between lawyers and clients can be affected by attitudes that result in negative behaviour, which is often driven by a lack of understanding and the overwhelming evidence present in a case. Furthermore, certain clients may expect their lawyers to show bias towards authorities in order to secure a favourable outcome in their cases. Individuals with misguided attitudes may need intervention from a higher power to facilitate genuine and lasting changes from within. It is not uncommon for humans to exhibit negative behaviour and hold innate wrong attitudes, often rooted in unresolved challenges or experiences from their early lives.

It is important to note that while the first man, Adam, and his wife chose to disobey God's laws and introduced sin into the world, this does not imply that individuals should strive for perfection. However, every person should behave responsibly and consistently acknowledge the significance of what Christ has done for them. Drawing an illustration from the analogy of a good fruit tree producing pleasant fruits compared to an evil tree producing bad fruits, one's attitude and personality can have clean motives, living transparently like looking into a mirror. What are your thoughts on this?

THE RIGHT ATTITUDE OF JESUS' PARENTS

When Jesus was a teenager, His parents followed the customary practice, according to the law, of visiting the temple in Jerusalem to attend the yearly feast. On this occasion recorded in Luke 2:41-52, they lost Him. Mary and Joseph, as loving parents, diligently searched everywhere but could not find Him. They asked among the crowd if anyone had seen Jesus but to no avail. They hoped to meet Him again at the place where they initially started and returned to Jerusalem to search for Him. It wasn't until late in the day that they found Jesus in a significant place, engaged in deep conversations and answering questions among notable individuals.

Jesus was sitting in the temple, disputing, teaching, and unveiling His Father's business. While many children His age would be playing games in the streets, Jesus reflected His priorities with a surprising and satisfying response to His parents. He asked, *'"Why were you searching for me?" he asked. 'Didn't you know I had to be in my Father's house?'" (Luke 2:49)*

Do you feel you have lost sight of Jesus? If so, respond to the urgent need to find Jesus by retracing where you began and reflecting on the events that transpired in between. Your spiritual journey is akin to your first encounter with Jesus, such as seeking His unfailing presence through communion, restored fellowship, and prayer. Jesus should be sought immediately, rather than living empty lives for extended periods without Him and the presence of the Holy Spirit. When you realise that Jesus is missing from your daily company, you should make all necessary efforts to search diligently and restore fellowship. His presence is right where you left Him. Individuals who have carelessly lost their comfort in Christ must diligently search until they find restoration in a right relationship with Him.

Making a firm decision to follow Jesus should be a positive desire, as He should always be present in your daily life. Remember His promise not to leave or forsake those who come to Him and willingly follow His way. The decision to follow Jesus may seem comfortable, but it often entails great cost and sacrifice with no earthly rewards or security.

Jesus, not having a home to call His own, told His disciples, *"Foxes have dens and birds have nests, but the Son of Man has nowhere to lay His head"* (Matthew 8:20). Humans, on the other hand, often focus on constructing grand mansions during their earthly lives. Yet, these dwellings are ultimately passed on to others, as there is no place for earthly possessions in the afterlife. Such possessions belong to others once we depart from this world. Everything pertains to the earthly realm, but your salvation guarantees a place in your heavenly abode. Have you made plans to reside there? May we strive to imitate Christ in all that we do, bringing glory to His name and reflecting His love to the world so that we may find ourselves there.

Four

Attitudes Towards Sinners

"**A**ll have sinned and fall short of the glory of God" (Romans 3:23). An individual who continues to engage in wrongdoing without repenting and accepting Jesus Christ as their Saviour is considered a sinner. They may choose to maintain the same company, affections, and language as other sinners until someone bears witness and shares their own salvation story.

The followers of Jesus Christ experienced a life of self-denial, which comes at a great cost. Each individual must be prepared and willing to make similar sacrifices. Following Jesus entails self-sacrifice. A genuine change in attitude and behaviour must take place within the individual. When communicating with sinners, speech should always be filled with grace, enabling you to answer each person with care. Never forget those who are suffering in bondage.

The life of a Christian believer is meant to be savoury and fragrant, although it may not always be characterised by grace. Our words and actions should be seasoned with grace, like salt, preserving our discourse and keeping it from corruption. However, we must also be aware that the old sinful nature and its desires tend to creep in and dominate the mind. It is through God's grace that we are saved from the alienation caused by sin.

Therefore, it is our duty to love people and offer encouragement for them to accept the free gift of salvation, which is freely offered to all. We should demonstrate compassion and prudence in our conduct towards the non-believing world, walking in wisdom among those who lack understanding. We must take care not to be harmed or harm others, nor should we increase their prejudices against other religions. Instead, we should make the most of every opportunity, walking circumspectly and avoiding any actions that could be used against us.

There is no better attitude to display towards people than love and compassion. We should remember that we were once in the same sinful condition, far from God and in need of a Saviour. Therefore, effectively winning the lost for Christ requires wise and Spirit-led witnessing. It necessitates understanding, grace, and providing clear answers to those who question your faith in Jesus Christ. All objections should be addressed politely, defending your faith and explaining the reasons behind it.

Christian believers have a duty to actively seek the lost and guide them towards the saving knowledge of Jesus Christ, the gospel. It is essential for them to hear the spoken word, accept it, believe in the Lord Jesus, and be saved. Salvation is not earned by our works but is a free gift from God, given by His grace through faith in Jesus Christ. Both faith and salvation are gifts from God, emphasising His grace (see Ephesians 2:8).

Salvation is not limited to a specific nation or group of people. While there may be instances where it appears that salvation is exclusive to Israel, God makes it clear that His purpose for salvation extends to the entire world. Those who have already accepted salvation should eagerly continue to seek more knowledge and actively strive to rescue others while there is still time. Christian believers are urged to go and win the lost at any cost. When reaching out to sinners, you can introduce salvation by making them aware that their salvation has already been bought and paid for through the death and resurrection of Jesus Christ.

Sinners should be encouraged by the fact that you too were once dead in trespasses and sins, but your soul was regenerated by the Holy Spirit, receiving new life. Christ saved sinners not because of their righteous deeds, but out of His merciful love, through the washing of the new birth and the renewal by the Holy Spirit, which is poured out generously through the blood of Jesus Christ. Therefore, believers should strive passionately to enter through the narrow door, persevering even though many will try but fail to enter (see Luke 13:24-25).

The narrow door symbolises Jesus Himself, as finding salvation requires concentrated efforts that many people are unwilling to make. No one can save themselves; it is only through God's grace that they can be saved. Believers must make the effort to guide others towards entering the narrow door, earnestly desiring to know Jesus, diligently striving to follow Him regardless of the cost. This decision should not be delayed because the door will not remain open indefinitely. We should adopt the attitude of the shepherd who left the ninety-nine sheep to search for the one that was lost.

Therefore, as Christians with a good attitude, we should actively seek out non-Christians, including those who have left the fellowship without reason or those who have become entangled in worldly activities. We need to have a passion for prodigals, understanding that it is an important principle in our ministry. By finding common ground and delicately approaching lost sinners and backsliders, we can help them in their weak and lonely state of mind, offering care and nurturing.

PRAYING FOR OTHERS EFFECTIVELY

Prayer is not merely a means to obtain personal desires; true prayer is about entering into God's presence and discovering His will for our lives. Therefore, when praying for the lost, it is important to engage in prayer with understanding. James addresses the common problem of misguided prayer, emphasising the significance of asking for the right things and for the right reasons. Instead of seeking to fulfill selfish desires or seeking God's approval for preconceived plans, our prayers become powerful when we allow God to change our hearts and align our desires with His will for us and for sinners (see James 4:3).

We can have confidence in God when we pray according to His will, knowing that He hears us. When we know that He hears our prayers, we can have assurance that our petitions will be answered (1 John 5:14-15). After praying, it is essential to invite new converts to join the local church, as it provides a nurturing environment for their spiritual growth. The church, which Jesus established on earth and purchased with His own blood, becomes victorious as the gospel is preached, leading people to believe in Jesus as the Son of God (1 John 5:5).

Saying, "I'm praying for you," brings comfort to others. Praying for the salvation of souls is a battle that we must not cease fighting until they come to the light of the world—Jesus. Prayer serves as the glue that connects people's hearts with their Creator. It should be a lifestyle for believers, as well as their duty and not an option. Prayer is not limited to converted sinners; it is relevant for everyone in the world. Although we may not fully comprehend the needs of each individual, the Holy Spirit knows their deepest desires, pain, and struggles. Thus, we should fervently pray for people everywhere, including those in positions of authority, the poor, the widows, and the repentant.

COMPASSIONATE PLEADING

Pleading for individuals entails making compassionate pleas for them to come to know and accept Jesus Christ as their Lord and Saviour. This task is not an easy one, as it requires deep concern and a battle against the powers of darkness. When pleading with sinners, it is crucial to approach them with a loving spirit and the right attitude. Patience and conviction are essential when sharing the gospel with those who may lack understanding or have negative attitudes towards it. The more we comprehend the meaning of the Bible and apply its teachings to our lives, the more impactful our words will be. In these moments, relying on the help of the Holy Spirit is crucial, as He assists us in presenting the gospel effectively and answering any objections or questions that may arise (see Acts 17:22-31).

Our genuine concern and nurturing attitude towards new believers will create an environment of love and support, where they feel encouraged to seek God wholeheartedly. By providing guidance and demonstrating Christ-like compassion, we can help them overcome challenges and build a strong foundation in their faith, ultimately leading to a life of fruitful Christian living that reflects God's grace and goodness to the world.

REBUKING WITH LOVE

When it comes to rebuking others, Christians must exercise caution and wisdom. It is important to choose the right time and place, avoiding public rebukes that may cause embarrassment. While *"open rebuke is better than secret love"* (Proverbs 27:5), it is crucial that rebuking is motivated by love. Rebuking someone should be done for the right reasons, showing how much you care about their well-being. Approach the situation with the right attitude, avoiding a controlling demeanor that may elicit negative reactions.

Misunderstandings often contribute to conflicts. When addressing past temptations or hurtful offenses, it is vital to remind others of God's forgiveness and the need to forgive and forget. Trust in God's forgiveness and seek a clear understanding of the situation. Reflect on how God has guided you, and let this perspective guide your actions. In times of prosperity, it is important not to forget God's past faithfulness. Express gratitude and acknowledge God as your source, despite negative opinions from others. Stay positive and trust that you will succeed.

The salvation of mankind is a free gift from God and cannot be earned or purchased. There may be times for rebuking and giving instruction, but it is essential to discern between truth and falsehood (Titus 1:10-13 AB).

ATTITUDE IN PERSUADING OTHERS

Believers who fear the Lord have the responsibility to persuade others about the impending judgment to come. This judgment is certain and universal, as all individuals will appear before the great Judge. The fear of the Lord, deeply rooted in the Scriptures, denotes a profound reverence for God. Therefore, individuals must be fully persuaded in their own faith before they can effectively share their experiences and persuade others to change their negative attitudes to positive thinking. When people heard Jesus teaching effectively, they were persuaded to follow Him and experience life transformation. Jesus said to His disciples, *"Whoever wants to be my disciple must deny themselves and take up their cross and follow me. For whoever wants to save their life will lose it, but whoever loses their life for me will find it."* (Matthew 16:24-25)

As Jesus went about on His journey, a man expressed his desire to follow Him wherever He went. However, Jesus told the man to go and share the message of God's kingdom with others instead of physically following Him (see Luke 9:57-62). This tells us that we are called to follow His example, not because we want to be in with the in-crowd or desire status. Jesus rebuked his disciples for disputing among themselves about who would be the greatest. He reminded them that ambition, honour, strife, and superiority are sins that stem from corrupt desires, which need to be subdued and mortified. While some individuals believe that making the right decision is enough, time will reveal the person's true needs that may hinder their efforts to persuade others. It is crucial for Christians to avoid the company of scandalous individuals who claim to be brethren but engage in fornication, idolatry, or slander. They should refrain from familiarising themselves with such people, even avoiding eating with them, to prevent any association that may bring shame to repentance.

The example of Moses persuading the people of Israel serves as a reminder. Moses consistently pleaded with them to remember the true and living God, His mercies, and His abundance as they travelled through the wilderness. Moses urged the people to change their attitudes, giving glory to God, and cautioned against negative pride. He warned them that as their material wealth increased, their minds would be prone to self-conceit, self-complacency, and self-confidence. Moses emphasised the importance of not forgetting God and following His commandments. He recounted their experiences in the wilderness, emphasising how God led them through perilous situations, provided water from rocks, and gave them manna to eat. All these trials were meant to humble and test them, reminding them that their prosperity was not the result of their own abilities but a gift from God.

In effect, Moses told them, "Look back and remind yourselves of the wilderness where God led you through. Remember how you were under strict discipline, what the wilderness life was like. It was like being in a school, spending a period of forty years boarded and being taught under unreasonable tutors and governors. God chastened you with the rod so that you would not be condemned. He wanted to teach you, like a good father who wants the best for his children. The method God used to train you was for His own purpose, mercy, and compassion."

How easy it is to take God's protection for granted! You seldom take notice or thank God when your car doesn't break down, your clothes don't rip, or your tools don't break. How different your attitude changes in times of plenty. It is incredibly easy for your prosperity to make you proud, believing that your own hard work and cleverness made you rich. While you are busy collecting and managing wealth, you push God out of your life. Just remember, God gives everything, and He only asks you to manage it for Him.

Having a loyal attitude is essential for believers. Their first loyalty should be to God, their Creator, in whom they live and have their being. Seeking the kingdom of God and His righteousness should take precedence, and God will provide for their needs. Loyalty to God means turning to Him for help, aligning one's thoughts with His desires, and embodying His character. Believers must consider what is truly important to them and how much loyalty Jesus demands. Stating the rewards for doing this, Jesus said, *"But whoever denies Me before men, him I will also deny before My Father who is in heaven"* (Matthew 10:33 NKJV).

It is possible to veer off course and become too focused on something or someone other than God. When our loyalty is misplaced or excessively directed towards worldly pursuits, ambitions, or individuals, it can lead us away from our true devotion to God. It is important to continually examine our hearts and priorities, ensuring that our loyalty remains steadfast to God above all else. *"For who makes you different from anyone else? What do you have that you did not receive? And if you did receive it, why do you boast as though you did not?"* (1 Corinthians 4:7)

True loyalty to God should not be coerced but freely given from a willing heart. It involves using one's life and resources to carry out God's desires rather than personal ambitions. Loyalty should not be based on force or favouritism but on love and faithfulness. Love and faithfulness are demonstrated through actions, and true friendship is proven by loyalty and support in times of distress. Believers should evaluate whether their actions align with their attitudes and strive to be loyal friends who love at all times. The Bible encourages genuine friendship that stands the test of time.

WHAT KIND OF FRIEND ARE YOU?

There is a contrast between true friendship and fake friendship. The greatest evidence of genuine friendship is loyalty and love at all times. A loyal friend makes themselves available to help in times of distress or struggle. While some friendships are short-lived and based on convenience or personal gain, true friendship goes beyond that.

In order to be a loyal friend, one must not only feel love but also act in a loyal and responsible manner. Likewise, a faithful person not only believes the truth but also seeks justice for others. It is not enough for your thoughts and words to reflect loyalty; your actions must also align with your attitudes. The true test of faithfulness in friendship is whether you love at all times.

To improve your loyalty to God, consider that your first allegiance belongs to Him. Seek opportunities to share your faith, help others in need, and stand up for justice. Use your life and resources to fulfill God's desires rather than your own. Remember that everything you have is a gift from God, and He asks you to manage it for His purposes.

Five

Attitudes Towards The World

Even though the world is vast and seemingly overwhelming, Christians should not feel lost or insignificant. Instead, they have the opportunity to shine brightly and make a positive impact by demonstrating the right attitude towards all people. By embodying Christ-like attitudes and values, they can make a meaningful difference in the lives of those around them and be a beacon of light in a dark world. God loves the entire world and gave His only begotten Son so that whoever believes in Him shall have everlasting life. This emphasises how much Christians should value the world, especially as followers of Christ. While it may not be wise for Christians to choose certain kinds of people as bosom friends, they are still expected to be God's hands and feet in offering help to those who do not know Christ. They are urged to distance themselves from the world's attitudes and systems and instead put on the character of Christ. In the times before their conversion, their desires were focused on fulfilling worldly things and the lust of the flesh. However, with the light of God's grace, they have been saved by grace, a gift from God.

The grace that saves sinners is the undeserved goodness and favour of God. Both their salvation and faith are gifts from God. God has a good, pleasing, and perfect will for their lives, desiring their transformation into new creatures through the renewal of their minds and obedience. The lingering feeling of self-gratitude and selfish desires that fight against their new attitude have been put to death. Christians, as followers of Christ Jesus, who justifies and enables believers to live a righteous life, should be faithful to God and present themselves as holy, serving as channels through which the righteousness of God is manifested and appeals to others.

The Apostle Paul wrote a statement from a heart of love and concern for Christians, appealing to them and urging them to make a decisive decision by dedicating their bodies, presenting all their members and faculties as living sacrifices, holy, devoted, consecrated, and well-pleasing to God (see Romans 12:1). Believers are the light of the world and should not yoke themselves with unbelievers. Instead, they should present their bodies as temples of the living God, recognising that there can be no agreement between the temples of God and the temples of idols. They are called to come out from among them and be separated, avoiding association with unclean things, just as one avoids the society of leprosy (see Romans 12:2).

DO NOT CONFORM WITH THE WORLD

There are valuable written guidelines regarding conforming to or engaging in things that are contrary to God's commands. Although Christians live in a sinful world, they should not engage in or adapt to the customs of the world. It is wrong for good people to join themselves with those who show affinity with the wicked. Instead of conforming to the world, Christians are called to be transformed and changed by the renewal of their minds, adopting a new ideal and attitude. By doing so, they can prove for themselves *"what is the good, acceptable, and perfect will of God"*, aligning themselves with what is good, acceptable, and perfect in His sight (see Romans 12:2).

What agreement is there between light and darkness? Conforming to the world means refusing to take part in or to support worldly activities, resisting being molded by the present thinking, value system, and conduct of the world. Christian believers are expected not to conform to the pattern of this world in their behaviour and customs, as they are usually self-centred. The ultimate purpose is to love God, who gave His only Son to make their lives new. Therefore, Christians should humble themselves under His control and righteousness, enabling them to conduct themselves with humility. They are encouraged to stand firm for Christ, not conforming in any way to unbelievers but keeping their eyes on Christ and remembering that this world is not their own.

The young church at Antioch was a curious mixture of Jews and Gentiles. It was significant as the first place believers were called Christians, as all they had in common was Christ, not race, culture, or language. It is important to understand that Christ alone can cross all boundaries and unite all races of people. Christians should not conform, settle, or agree with the world system without examining its course and the attitude of carelessness that comes with compromising with the system of the world. Can an individual play with fire and not expect to get burned?

Christians have hope that God will one day transform their lowly bodies into glorious bodies like Christ's. Unfortunately, in this life, they may struggle with physical limitations and disabilities of all sorts. However, they can look forward with hope to the resurrection and the promise of a new body. In the present world, some may devote excessive time and effort to enhancing their bodies, adorning them or barely dressing them. They may not realise that their bodies will one day return to dust, but believers in Christ will receive new bodies.

The God of mercy and justice personally cares for each of His followers, expecting them to imitate and follow His high moral standards. This includes giving others the time they are unable to give themselves and focusing on the heavenly standard of holiness. Believers are called to be holy and fully dedicated to God, set apart for special use. They can be set apart without blending in with the crowd, yet not being different just for the sake of being different. It involves realising that God's qualities are operating in their lives and seeking to conduct themselves in holiness. They should not be concerned with pleasing men but instead prioritise God's purpose (see Galatians 1:10 and Acts 5:29).

NOT LOVING THE WORLD

"If anyone loves the world, the love of the Father is not in him" (1 John 2:15). Worldliness is described as internal and begins in the heart. It is characterised by three attitudes: the lust of the flesh

(physical desires), the lust of the eyes (craving and accumulating things), and the pride of life (self-interests). Temptation follows these patterns and appeals to these three fundamental areas of life. That is why individuals are prone to various experiences of temptation based on their strengths and weaknesses in these three areas. Satan caused the fall of man by appealing to these weaknesses, and he also tested Christ with these same temptations, relying on the authority of the Scriptures. However, Christ resisted and said, *"You shall not tempt the Lord your God."* (Matthew 4:7)

If Christians find themselves loving the world, it signifies that they are enjoying the ungodliness present in the world. Even small or great things can become gods, demanding worship and possible sacrifices. The Word of God warns against the love and worship of other gods and advises believers to be aware.

This does not mean disliking a person; rather, it means that the love of God is not in that person. It is possible for individuals not to be like others due to a selfish attitude that entices them to ignore and mistreat others, seeing them as irritants, competitors, or enemies. Those who love the world will inevitably participate in the world's system. While some believers see worldliness as limited to external behaviour, using the excuse that man looks at the outward appearance but God sees the heart, it is wrong to judge others and deny the truth. The people one associates with, the places one attends, and the activities one enjoys can be indicators of an attitude focused on worldly pleasures. Some believers choose to dress like the people of the world, wearing revealing attire that expresses wrong behaviour. Can you imagine what the world is thinking and mocking when a Christian behaves this way? How can one introduce Jesus to the people of the world while engaging in such actions? Listen to the Word of God as a warning: "B*ut whoever keeps His word, truly the love of God is perfected in him. By this, we know that we are in Him.*" (1 John 2:15 NKJV)

NOT FRIENDLY WITH THE WORLD

Friendship with the world is hostility against God. While friends naturally share love, sympathy, and make sacrifices, comparing Christian love with the world reveals that it's not merely a feeling but a choice. Therefore, one must make positive choices for the well-being of others, treat them with respect, and avoid developing unhealthy attachments or falling into unholy relationships.

While some argue that worldliness extends beyond external behaviour to include places, activities, and associations, others believe that it is possible for individuals to maintain deep friendships based on their shared commitment to God and each other without compromising their faith.

It is true that conflicts may arise when beliefs clash, and it is important for Christians to remain steadfast in their loyalty to God and His principles. This may require making difficult choices and separating from relationships or activities that contradict their faith. However, it is also possible for individuals to build strong friendships with those who may not share the same beliefs but respect and support each other's convictions.

Ultimately, the key is to discern the impact of our associations and friendships on our faith and to ensure that our loyalty to God remains unwavering. While it's not wrong to desire a pleasurable life, seeking pleasure at the expense of others or disobeying God is part of being friendly with the world. Worldly pleasures often divert individuals from pleasing God. It's important to consider which side one is on: serving God if He is God or choosing the world if it offers what one desires. This includes refraining from attending places of entertainment, listening to worldly music, and engaging in illicit activities. It is important to seek wisdom and guidance from God, study His Word, and surround ourselves with positive influences that strengthen our commitment to Him. Multiple reasons exist for not loving the world and its attractions. Due to human fallen nature, there is a tendency to revert to old habits and slip back into the ways of the world. Therefore, the call is to separate oneself from the world to please God (James 1:27).

AVOID LUSTING FOR WORLDLY THINGS

The lust of the flesh comes in various forms and can entice the eyes. Opening one package of worldly desires can lead to the manifestation of other destructive attitudes and behaviours. This behaviour can even affect spiritual leaders, and one should avoid elevating them to a position of pride that causes division among the body of Christ. Instead, recognise that each preacher is a humble servant who has suffered for the message of Jesus Christ, and no preacher holds more status than another (1 Corinthians 4:7).

Believers should never allow negative thoughts and lustful desires to stir up unbelief, strife, slander, or other attitudes that break relationships. The right attitude should always be drawn from the example of Christ rather than human agents. Negative attitudes and fleshly behaviours have a long history of destruction, driven by evil desires. Instead, one should follow the guidance of the Holy Spirit and possess the power to resist fleshly desires. The unhealthy desires of the flesh require strict attention and must be put to death, including sexual immorality, witchcraft, selfish ambition, hatred, and jealousy. Believers should not conform to the evil desires of the world or live as they once did in ignorance. The One who calls them is holy, so they should strive to be holy in all they do.

ABUSING AUTHORITY

Abusing authority involves misusing power or causing physical harm and insults to others. Those in positions of authority should never use their power for wrongful purposes or abuse and mistreat others. Negative behaviour and abuse are prevalent in society, seen both in the world system's perversion of the truth and individuals treating others crudely. This can manifest in brashness, intimidation, ridicule, harassment, or treating adults as children.

Individuals in authority should never abuse the trust, loyalty, or faith of those who look to them as servants of God. The brutality and selfish behaviour of abusers are pervasive in society. Even children often experience abuse from those who should be caring for them, and parents can abuse one another. The world is plagued with people abusing one another, causing significant damage until authorities must intervene to rescue victims.

NOT ENTANGLED WITH

The world may wonder about the cause of entanglement. Entanglement occurs when one becomes twisted or caught up in something, much like a fish swimming through a mesh and getting entangled, making it difficult to break free. Similarly, individuals can experience emotional struggles where their minds are unable to fully decide what they want, caught in an internal struggle between what is right and what the heart desires. This can be broken by the power of the Holy Spirit. When boundaries are violated, relationships become blurred, resulting in a broken relationship with God. It is in this context that a loving call from the Word of God instructs us.

"Stand fast therefore in the liberty by which Christ has made us free, and do not be entangled again with a yoke of bondage" (Galatians 5:1 NKJV). When it comes to unholy behaviour, we are advised not to conform any longer to the pattern of this world. Instead, we are to be transformed by the renewing of our minds, enabling us to test and approve what is pleasing to God. We are to stand firm in the liberty that Christ has set us free, avoiding once again being subject to the yoke of bondage. The freedom from the law allows us to retain spiritual freedom, as under the gospel, we are brought into a state of liberty.

We must be cautious and avoid getting entangled in relationships from which we cannot break free. Sin, like an entangling monster, grips anyone in its path, tying and entangling them with its works. Only the blood of Jesus can free us from its hold. Sin can indeed be deceptive and have a gradual influence on individuals, even those who consider themselves intelligent, independent, or worldly wise. It is common for people to underestimate the power of sin and its ability to entice and ensnare.

Sometimes, individuals may believe they are too wise or strong to be easily tempted or swayed by the habits and attitudes of the world. However, this sense of self-assurance can lead to complacency and a vulnerability to the subtle influences of sin. For instance, an enemy may come near, acting friendly with good intentions, wrapping themselves around us as if harmless until we realise the true danger. Likewise, the allure of worldly pleasures, materialism, selfishness, and other sinful behaviours can gradually erode one's moral compass and draw them away from their faith and godly principles.

It is important for individuals to recognise their own susceptibility to sin and guard against it by staying rooted in their relationship with God, regularly examining their attitudes and behaviours, and seeking accountability and support from fellow believers. Humility and a constant reliance on God's strength and guidance are crucial in resisting the pull of sin and maintaining a life that is aligned with His will.

It is because of our falleness that all human liberty is owed to Christ, who has made us free. It is our duty to stand firm in this liberty and not allow ourselves to be entangled once again in the yoke of bondage. It requires having a mindset to give up worldly securities and enduring rigorous discipline, just like athletes who train extremely hard, following the rules to win the race. Farming is an apt demonstration of this for it requires working extremely hard, enduring the heat of the day, with the hope of a good crop on the day of harvest. We too must work, striving for enduring and worthwhile achievements that glorify

God and bring people to Christ. On that day, we will enjoy eternity with Him.

Similarly, to walk safely at night, we need a light to prevent tripping over broken pavements and tree roots or falling into potholes, as if walking through a dark forest of evil. The Bible serves as our light, showing us the way ahead, preventing us from stumbling, and revealing the entangling roots of false values and philosophies of the world. Reading and studying the Bible help us see our path clearer and enable us to stay on the right track.

DEFILEMENT, THE PROCESS OF MAKING IMPURE

Defilement refers to making something pure impure. It can cause damage to purity or appearance, similar to marking or spoiling. God keeps believers from falling, regardless of what the unbelievers do or how successful they may seem by worldly standards. However, there are written warnings in God's word regarding the wrath to come. It is a matter of life and death, and therefore, believers must share the message of salvation with those they meet. We must be cautious about falling into the quicksand of corruption and also examine our own attitudes of transparency.

Defilement can manifest in various ways, such as speech, attire, listening to worldly music, watching inappropriate films, paying too much attention to the wrong things, craving unholy desires, and believing that it's alright. Although it may seem easy to handle, we should never trust ourselves, as sin can mask itself like a snake. Eventually, that snake will crawl and strike unexpectedly, revealing the real danger. We must be extremely careful as the devil's tactics are not to be taken lightly. He is like a roaring lion but can also appear harmless, violating the chastity and purity of individuals. Defilement entails being spiritually unclean and comes from failing to avoid unpleasant or contaminating things that can taint a person. Jesus presented a list of defiling elements, affirming that it is not what enters our bodies that defiles us, but rather what emanates from within our hearts. Evil thoughts, murders, adultery, fornication, theft, false witness, and blasphemy are the actions and attitudes that defile an individual.

GUARDING AGAINST DEFILEMENT

Believers must be extremely careful not to allow anything or anyone to defile their character. Bitterness, if left unchecked, can grow and overshadow even the closest relationships. It starts as a small root but can grow into a large tree. Therefore, believers must avoid getting mixed up in worldly standards. It is not Christ-like to conform to worldly standards as believers. *"Now to Him who is able to keep you from stumbling or falling into sin, and to present you unblemished [blameless and faultless] in the presence of His glory with triumphant joy and unspeakable delight"* (Jude 24).

Although believers are no longer bound by the Old Testament restrictions related to defilement from touching dead bodies or dealing with leprosy, they must still adhere to the spiritual manifestations of defilement. The worst form of defilement that can happen to a Christian is defiling their conscience. Such a conscience becomes dead and unable to weigh rightly. Instead, believers should have a lively conscience that discerns between right and wrong in their own actions. They should avoid touching, tasting, or handling things that would defile their bodies, just as they should avoid sin. When we meddle with the actions and principles of the world, we become contaminated.

AVOIDING CONFORMITY TO THE WORLD

Christian believers are called not to conform any longer to the behaviour and customs of the world. Worldly customs often prioritise self-satisfaction and corruption. Simply avoiding bad behaviour on the surface is not enough; transformation must occur at a deeper level in our minds. Our minds should be renewed, moving away from our old sinful ways and embracing the new life in Jesus Christ. Salvation and eternal life with God cannot be earned through human achievements. Following Jesus requires self-sacrifice, and we must be willing to count the cost and follow in obedience. We should always strive to please God rather than seek approval from the world. Similar to the Apostle Paul, who never sought to please the world but instead aimed to please God, we should live our lives in a way that pleases Him. It is essential to have genuine concern for others and be willing to help, just as a loving parent would for their children. While the world may honour intelligence, beauty, wealth, and power, our focus should be on being kind to others, acknowledging the importance of their feelings, and creating opportunities for harmonious relationships. We should never judge others based on their spirituality, fulfillment of duties, or human activities, as only God knows the inner thoughts of individuals.

FORSAKING ALL FOR CHRIST'S SAKE

What does the Bible say about forsaking all for Christ's sake? Forsaking means to abandon or leave behind. For example, forsaking all others for the sake of one person at the marriage altar means dedicating oneself solely to that person and not allowing any room for others. Similarly, when we come to Christ, we must forsake all other idols and focus our hearts and minds on the things of God.

To forsake means to put out of sight and denounce anything that competes with Christ as Lord and Master. It involves pursuing a love for worship and avoiding worldly company that may lead to backsliding. Instead, we should strive to make progress in our Christian lives, seeking after what is good and pleasing to God.

One of the challenges of following Christ is accepting and sharing in His suffering, forsaking all for Him. God's love is not limited by the amount of suffering we endure. Romans 8:28 teaches us that nothing can separate us from God. While we may have personal goals, if we exclude God from our plans, we will never truly achieve them. When we live for Him and seek His will, He will align our plans with His, leading us to fulfillment and never disappointing us.

Throughout history, people have searched for a fountain of youth or a source of eternal life and vitality, but such things were never found. However, God's wisdom is a fountain of life that brings happiness, health, and eternal life. The living Word of God has the power to wash away the deadly effects of sin and give us hope for eternity while transforming our present lives.

The Holy Spirit assists believers in forsaking the works of the flesh and being accountable in their walk with God. Jesus taught that whoever seeks to save their life will lose it, but those who lose their life for His sake will find it. This means that true life is found in surrendering ourselves completely to Christ and His purposes.

When it comes to serving Christ, individuals may need to make different choices about what to give up. This may include bad habits, desires of the heart, places of pleasure, negative attitudes, wrong company, or poor decision-making. While Jesus demands wholehearted commitment, His standard of righteousness is attainable through His grace and with the help of the Holy Spirit.

If we choose to be saved, it is only by God's grace and not by our own efforts. It is a gift from God through Jesus Christ. Jesus invites us to take His yoke, which is easy and His burden, which is light. A yoke was a heavy wooden harness used on oxen. In this context, it represents the burdens of sin, religious oppression, and weariness. Jesus offers freedom from these burdens and promises love, healing, peace with God, and purpose in life.

Forsaking sinful desires means actively avoiding and running away from sin. Even a little sin can be a destructive force. Christians are called to avoid anything unclean and every form of evil. When we are polluted by sin and compromise our witness, we cannot effectively serve in ministry or use our time well.

Another significant aspect of forsaking all for Christ's sake is the wise use of our time. Time is precious and cannot be retraced, replaced, or regained. We should carefully steward our time, recognising that there is a time for everything under the sun. While some may choose to give up certain things during the season of Lent, God desires our total commitment at all times.

Attitudes Towards Loving God

The dictionary provides various definitions of the word "love", such as a feeling of warm personal attachment or deep affection for a friend, parent, or child. It can also refer to a warm fondness or liking for another person, as well as the benevolent affection of God for His creatures and the reverent affection due from them to God. Love can be further defined as the kindly affection properly expressed by God's creatures towards one another. This type of love can be strong or passionate, particularly when it comes to a romantic attraction that serves as the emotional incentive for conjugal union. However, love for God can only be truly effective after accepting the Lord Jesus as Saviour and Lord.

The Holy Spirit's work teaches individuals how to love God and love people, as without His guidance, one would be unable to love as they ought. Jesus states that whoever has His commandments and obeys them is the one who loves Him. He promises that those who love Him will be loved by His Father, and He Himself will love them and reveal Himself to them. It is crucial for individuals to have the right attitude in loving God, not simply for what they can gain from Him. True love for God acknowledges that He is the Creator who knows one's frame, and recognises our helplessness and need for a Saviour.

Followers of Christ should demonstrate their love for Him through obedience, as mere words of commitment and conduct are not enough. If one loves Christ, they should prove it by obeying His word, loving Him with all their heart, soul, and mind, and showcasing a devoted love that cannot easily be swayed by external influences. Instead, they should remain determined, maintaining the right attitude and staying committed to the course, even when faced with sacrifice and unconventional circumstances. This type of love requires wholehearted belief in God and God alone.

God's love for the human race is immeasurable and cannot be limited by the degree of suffering one may experience. Romans 8:38-39 teaches that nothing can separate individuals from God's love. While they may have many goals to achieve, excluding God from their plans will hinder their ability to attain true fulfillment. However, if they include God in their lives, He will intervene and rearrange their plans, enabling them to live for Him. When their earthly journey ends, they will have fulfilled their plans because God is faithful and never disappoints.

In the Gospel of Matthew, chapter 22, verses 34-40, Jesus is asked by a Pharisee lawyer about the greatest commandment in the Law. Jesus responds by saying, "You shall love the Lord your God with all your heart, with all your soul, and with all your mind. This is the first and greatest commandment." In this powerful statement, Jesus emphasises the paramount importance of our love and devotion to God. He calls us to wholeheartedly give ourselves to Him, aligning our thoughts, emotions, and actions in complete allegiance to the One who created and loves us unconditionally. By loving God above all else, we find the foundation for a meaningful and purposeful life, honouring the very essence of our existence.

Love represents freedom from sin. The law was introduced to increase awareness of trespasses, but where sin increased, God's grace increased even more (see Romans 5:20). As sinners, separated from God, humans view His law as a ladder to be climbed in order to reach Him. However, countless attempts to ascend that ladder without the help of God Himself have led to failure and disappointment. We must climb with the Holy Spirit. Despite the overwhelming height of the ladder, we can then approach it with boldness and positivity, understanding that if we stumble, we will not fall to the ground. Instead, we will be caught and held in God's hands.

LOVE LIFE

One's personal attitude towards life should be positive, acknowledging that life cannot be purchased or saved up with money. Life is a free gift given by the Creator to humanity. It originates from the breath of God, and its meaning stems from being made in His image. While life may seem fleeting, described as a dream that vanishes like a vision of the night, it belongs to the people of God. A good life, filled with inner peace, calmness, assurance, and joy, is available to anyone who is a child of God through Jesus Christ. This kind of life is characterised by a right attitude and can be experienced even in the midst of challenging circumstances. Life is like a vapor, short and unpredictable, and should not be postponed, thinking there is enough time to serve the Lord.

Eternal life can be enjoyed on earth here and now, providing real peace, knowledge, and lasting joy. These elements contribute to a beautiful life, desired by God for His children. Life is not merely meant for personal happiness and fulfillment but for serving and honouring God. The worth and meaning of life is not subject to the world's perspective, but on the way of the Spirit. No one can take this life away, as it comes from the immutability of God love for His creation. This does not mean that we avoid suffering but we can trust that God will always give us the ability to stand secure in Him. The written Word of God holds immeasurable value, and He understands that life cannot truly be beautiful without stability. True stability is not based on material possessions or worldly achievements but on the fear of the Lord and reverent obedience to Him. A life-changing relationship through trusting in Christ as a personal Saviour is essential. Again, merely knowing and obeying the truth is not enough; it requires genuine belief and adherence to God's will. The birth, life, death, resurrection, and second coming of Jesus Christ are historical events that provide the foundation for a good life.

Life is like a shadow that will fly away, similar to a dream (see Job 20:8), but God's everlasting nature surpasses the fleeting lives of humanity. Nothing will last unless it is rooted in God's unchanging character and so finding anything permanent requires a relationship with God. In times of deep anguish and bitterness, individuals should call out to God in prayer, gaining an eternal perspective that helps them deal with each moment in the name of Jesus. A person will find that although the fountain of youth is nothing more than a dream, the fountain of life is a reality. With the choice to be enlightened by God's wisdom, individuals can rise above their own foolishness and avoid being weighed down.

In the book of Hebrews, believers regarded long life as a sign of God's blessings. Gray hair and old age were considered good. Younger people often rely on their strength, but the truth is that old age brings the experience and practical wisdom worth rejoicing over. Gray hair is not a sign of disgrace; rather, it is a crown of splendour. When interacting with older people, respect and compassion should be shown, allowing the Word of God to bring about positive changes, transforming negative attitudes into a positive outlook. It is important to listen to others, even the simplest person, as their advice may prove useful later on. The knowledge of God's will is useless unless it is lived out; merely knowing and obeying the truth is not enough. People mature in age have more experience in this wise, even though we know that age does not necessarily always equate with wisdom.

PRESERVE LIFE

Normally, humans seek to preserve something that is special to them, taking necessary measures to keep it safe from harm and danger. They ensure it remains warm, comfortable, and up to a high standard. Various methods of preservation exist, such as using a deep freezer to keep food fresh for an extended period or employing different techniques to preserve meat and fish. While individuals can choose from different preservation methods, only God has the authority to preserve human life.

Seeking God's face is the key to preserving one's own life and the lives of others. God's miracles often involve the spiritual side of human nature, opening the spiritual eyes of those lacking perception for spiritual truth and allowing the spiritually deaf to hear His message. He grants His people spiritual discernment and the ability to comprehend truths about Himself and as He does so, His Word preserves.

God commands us to love Him because He knows that in loving Him, we find true nourishment for our souls. By putting God first in our hearts, minds, and souls, we align ourselves with His will and purpose for our lives. We invite God's blessings, protection, and guidance upon us. Loving God wholeheartedly leads us to a life that is deeply fulfilling and spiritually enriching. Through this love, we experience God's sustaining grace, abundant provision, and the promise of eternal life with Him.

A story is told of a man who was travelling on board a ship with his fellow passengers. The sea became rough, posing a life-threatening situation. The man sought to preserve the lives of everyone on board during this stormy weather. However, the captain of the ship wanted to avoid spending the winter in a certain place, so they took a chance and decided to take an alternate route. Despite being warned of the danger ahead, they continued the journey. At first, the weather seemed favourable, but soon a deadly storm arose, forcing the crew to take drastic measures for survival, such as passing ropes under the ship to hold it together.

The crew had initially disregarded advice from a less significant member who was a prisoner on board. They did not consider his advice credible. Only when trouble struck and the storm raged did they listen to him. Sometimes, individuals express a wrong attitude towards a problem and refuse to accept advice from anyone but themselves. It is important to be open to listening to even the simplest person because their advice, though it may not make sense at the time, might prove useful later on. In this story, the crew was emphatically encouraged that the voyage would not result in any danger to their lives. You might recall this story as it is the one told of Paul in Acts 27:4 to 28:5. They were told, *"not one of you will be lost; only the ship will be destroyed"* (Acts 27:22).

Though things may be lost, the preservation of one's soul is paramount, as people are more valuable than possessions. It is essential to listen to advice and not stubbornly pursue one's own way. In the shipwreck story, Paul admonished those onboard, saying, "You should have listened and not set sail in this manner," as the Spirit had warned. Nonetheless, the crew was grateful that God showed compassion to them despite the predicament they brought upon themselves. Although the ship was destroyed, the lives of the crew were saved. This scenario is reflective of today's society, where individuals whose lives have been shattered by sin, distress, disappointment, and other atrocities can be restored and set sail again, even amidst the brokenness. Even if something seems impossible, the Word of God assures that *"with God all things are possible"* (Luke 18:27).

Seven

Attitudes Aproaching God

The right attitude to approach God is by rendering reverence, honour, and homage as true worship to the Creator. It should reflect every aspect of a person's life. The Hebrew word conveying the idea of worship, "avid", basically means to serve. Thus, worshipping God requires obedience to all His commands and doing His will, being exclusively devoted to Him. The death and resurrection of Christ have allowed us to worship God freely. The Bible says, "...through whom we have gained access by faith into this grace in which we now stand. And we boast in the hope of the glory of God." (Romans 5:12)

Individuals who genuinely love God should never hesitate to approach Him in prayer. They can come with confidence, understanding that their ability to do so does not rely on their own strength alone, but through Jesus, the great high priest. There are two distinct ways of approaching God that can be identified: approaching Him as a means of reconciling a broken relationship and approaching Him as a way of building a new one. When we approach God, it is essential to do so with a combination of confidence, reverence, and gratitude. While humility and surrendering to His will are crucial, they do not diminish the importance of having confidence. Throughout the Bible, we witness various examples of men approaching God in different ways.

When God created Adam, He did not prescribe a particular ceremony or means by which perfect man might approach Him in worship. Nevertheless, before the fall, Adam served and worshipped his Creator by faithfully doing the will of his heavenly Father. True worship is the basis of praise, describing God's character and attributes in the presence of others. As members of the body of Christ, we recognise and affirm His goodness, holding up His perfect moral nature for all to see, so that others may desire to know and accept His invitation as Saviour and Lord. When we approach God in praise, it has an effective spiritual benefit that helps us take our minds off our problems and needs, allowing us to focus on His power, mercy, and majesty.

True love for God desires true worship from the heart, lifting clean hands and having a pure heart. The Psalmist says in holy joy, *"Ascribe to the Lord the glory due his name; bring an offering and come before him. Worship the Lord in the splendor of his holiness"* (1 Chronicles 16:29). Genuine praise also involves ascribing glory to God. Whatever we offer to God, we should do it with all our hearts.

When individuals approach God, they must do so with reverence, prayerfully, and with godly fear, realising that God is not equal to mere man. God is the highest, above all other gods, yet He can be touched by our feelings. God knows our human frame is frail and our finite minds are unable to comprehend His holy standard. Although God created man in His likeness, man should not take God's mercy and grace for granted. We ought to develop and maintain a positive attitude when approaching and coming near to Him. Approaching God's presence for salvation, rest, and promises should be done with a prayerful attitude and by abiding in His presence. God is our friend, Sovereign Lord, Mighty God, Everlasting Father, Prince of Peace, Conquering Lion of the tribe of Judah, defense, fortress, battle-axe, deliverer, and so much more. Glory to God!

To give praise to the Most High God is to focus on His character and attributes. As members of the body of Christ, we recognise His mercies and affirm His goodness. As His creation, we worship and adore Him because He is worthy. Worship should not be based on emotions alone but on His power, knowledge, and infinite attributes.

In the Old Testament, approaching God was hindered by the middle wall of partition, which separated people from God due to their sinfulness. However, in the New Testament, when Jesus died on the cross and was resurrected, He removed that barrier and redeemed mankind from sin. Through His forgiveness, we can now approach God with the right attitude and a good spirit when we accept the free offer of salvation and know God through His Son, Jesus.

Approaching God requires a positive attitude and understanding of His nature, as well as avoiding things that displease Him. It is important to approach God with godly fear, which means respecting and honouring Him, demonstrating true reverence through our attitude and genuine worship. Examples of reverence and awe towards God can be seen in the lives of Abraham and Moses.

Abraham demonstrated his reverence for God when he obediently followed God's command to leave his homeland and go to a land that God would show him. Despite not knowing where he was going, Abraham trusted in God's guidance and had faith in His promises. In Genesis 12:4, it is stated, "*So Abram went, as the Lord had told him*". This act of obedience and trust displayed Abraham's deep reverence for God and his willingness to submit to His authority.

Moses also exhibited great reverence when he encountered God at the burning bush. In Exodus 3, Moses approached the burning bush with a sense of awe and humility. He took off his sandals, recognising the holiness of the ground on which he stood. In Exodus 3:6, it is written, "*Then he said, 'I am the God of your father, the God of Abraham, the God of Isaac, and the God of Jacob.' And Moses hid his face, for he was afraid to look at God.*" Moses' response of hiding his face revealed his deep reverence and acknowledgement of God's holiness and presence.

Both Abraham and Moses approached God with a profound sense of respect, recognising His authority and power. Their actions serve as examples of how we should approach God with humility, awe, and reverence. Reverence is not limited to sitting quietly in church but also includes obeying God in our speech and treating others with the right attitude.

When approaching God, it is essential not to do so frivolously or in a state of unbelief and lack of respect. Instead, we should come to Him with sincerity, honesty, and boldness. God encourages

His children to come to Him boldly and every day, accepting Him as the God who sent His Son to die for the world. Just as we respect and submit to our earthly fathers, we should show even more respect and submission to God the Father and the Holy Spirit.

RIGHT ATTITUDES

God extends a glorious invitation in Isaiah 1:18 when He beckons to all, saying, *"Come now, and let us reason together,"* and promising that though our sins may be like scarlet, He will make them white as snow. It is a privilege to come to God and find rest in Him. It is crucial to understand that God is not in the same league as man and to approach Him with the right attitude of understanding His greatness.

God does not necessarily make Himself known with the blast of a trumpet. Elijah experienced fatigue and discouragement after his victories and prayed earnestly for rain. God answered his prayer with a gentle whisper. This teaches us that God does not always reveal Himself in powerful and miraculous ways but can be encountered anywhere and at any time, whether in the valley or the mountain. We should always be attentive to His gentle whispering voice.

Worshipping God should be approached with a sacred attitude. Negative and unholy attitudes, as well as inappropriate behaviour and attire that draw attention away from true worship, should be avoided. God desires truthful worship in holiness and holy reverence, not a dull mourning attitude or a carnival-like display. Approaching God's presence through worship should be joyful, entering into His courts with thanksgiving and praise, with the expectation of having an audience with the King of glory and the Lord of lords.

Worshipping God should not be done reluctantly or as a mere ritual, but with thankfulness and an acknowledgement of His goodness and enduring mercies. Considering that we worship the King of kings and the Lord of lords, we should behave with reverence. If we were summoned to visit an earthly king, we would be on our best behaviour. Therefore, we should take even more thought and reverence when approaching Jehovah God, who is the Supreme Highest of all.

True worship of God is well-pleasing to Him, as He alone is worthy of worship. It is important to gain knowledge of the true and living God and to understand how to worship Him in spirit and in truth. The state of mind during worship is crucial, not just the object and manner of worship. God has given clear instructions for worshipping Him in spirit and in truth, and these instructions should not be debated.

Expressions of worship can encompass thoughts, feelings, and deeds. There are many ways to express worship to God, including praise, adoration, thanksgiving, and declaration. Worship can be expressed openly or publicly through joyful singing, reading the Bible silently, prayerfully acknowledging God's greatness and goodness, lifting hands and hearts, and celebrating His creation. Some may worship quietly, barely opening their mouths, but still be deeply connected to worshipping God.

When expressing true worship, it depends on the individual's personality and the setting. Whether in secret, at home, in public worship, or entering God's courts with praise, the sincere desire to worship God in all aspects is important. True worship begins from a clean and pure heart and permeates the atmosphere. The expression of worship may also include offering sacrifices of praise, confessing the name of Jesus, doing good, sharing with others, and giving thanks for Jesus' sacrifice on the cross, as well as sharing this message with others.

APPROACHING GOD WITH CONFIDENCE

In the Old Testament, David brought back the Ark of the Covenant to restore true worship. Worship was central to all Israel, and the temple stood as the throne of God on earth. True worship starts from acknowledging God as the true King over our lives. God ordained the priests and Levites to guide the people in faithful worship. David invited men, maidens, old men, and children to participate in worship and exalt the name of the Lord.

The privilege of immediate access to God is now available to all believers. We can approach God with confidence and receive mercy and help in times of need (Hebrews 4:16). Worshipping God is personal, as it involves having a personal relationship with Him. When gathered in the temple, the people of God were excited and engaged in their worship. Singing aloud and expressing joy and triumph were ways to praise God. Worshipping God should be done in all expressions of joy and praise, at any time, and with a warm and affectionate attitude. The dedication of the temple in the Old Testament symbolised setting it apart for an exclusive and purposeful worship. Similarly, believers are God's treasure, the apple of His eye, and the special object of His love. God cares for His people, provides for them, and has appointed them to live for His praise and glory.

God taught His people how to worship and emphasised sacrifice as a means of seeking forgiveness for sins. Sin separates people from God, and sacrifice was a way to restore the relationship. God made the ultimate sacrifice by sending His Son to die for humanity. Today, we are invited to have faith in this simple message as a means of access into this glorious relationship where we can worship the One who made us. Approaching God with a rightful attitude and accepting His forgiveness is therefore essential in worship.

FAMILY WORSHIP

The family was the first unit created by God, and through the family, God illustrates the visible relationship that exists between Christ and His church. It is believed that when a family prays together, they stay together, forming a strong and unbreakable unit. Family worship is typically led by the father, who is responsible as the head of the household. If the father is absent, the responsibility of leadership falls on the mother. The attitude of worship within the family is intended for instruction, correction, discipline, sharing love for God and others through the Holy Scriptures, observing His righteous acts, communion, and consecration.

In some homes of the people of Israel, a blessing is pronounced when the family gathers to worship God, creating an awe-inspiring spiritual atmosphere that draws the worshippers closer to each other in fellowship. Family worship is therapeutic for the entire family, especially when all members are present. Just as God chose Abraham because He knew that he would direct his children and household to keep the way of the Lord, it is important for those who desire family blessings to prioritise family worship. When children belong to the Lord, they must be nurtured for Him, and in turn, the Lord fulfills His promises as He did to Abraham (Genesis 18:19).

The ultimate purpose of parental discipline is to help and train children to grow in the fear of the Lord. Parenting is not an easy task, requiring patience in raising children to love and honour Christ. From birth to young adulthood, children need parental discipline, and parents are encouraged to provide it. However, a parent should not discipline their children with anger, frustration, hastiness, or impatience. Instead, parents should act in love, treating their children as Jesus treats the people He loves. This approach is vital for the child's development and for imparting important lessons that they will carry into adulthood. *"Honor your father and your mother—this is the first commandment with a promise"* (Ephesians 6:2).

Fathers are warned in the Holy Scriptures not to exasperate their children but rather to bring them up in the training and instruction of the Lord. The father of the home should be engaged in training children in the fear of the Lord, which is the beginning of wisdom. Each child will then become a testimony, bearing fruit and growing up like olive branches.

Praise and worship in the home are of utmost importance and should be acknowledged as a favour from God to be included in home worship services. Hebrew families took great pride in family worship, emphasising the significance of the entire family worshipping God together. Whether offering sacrifices or attending feasts, the family is encouraged to be together. There should be no excuses for not attending family gatherings. This tight-knit family relationship encourages the importance of worshipping Jehovah God from an early age.

Family principles instil respect and the right attitude towards worship, placing great emphasis on family members confessing the Lord and also confessing faults and failures to one another as an important part of celebrating holidays together. Although there may be appropriate times for separating people by age and gender, meaningful worship can be experienced when shared by people of all ages. This attitude should be taught from the beginning in homes, ensuring that as they grow older, they will not depart from it.

Many people in the world allow wrong attitudes and things to become gods in their lives without realising it until it is too late. The wrong attitude of giving worship to something or someone may soon develop deep love for false worship, self-adoration, and an excessive focus on personal identity, money, fame, achievements, or the desire for acknowledgement. These little monsters can grow into gods and ultimately control thoughts and attitudes. The truth is, it is necessary to ask for God's help and to allow Him to take centre stage in one's life, which will put one back on the straight and narrow path. The problem began when God said to the people, *"You shall have no other god besides me"* (Exodus 20:3). It was the first commandment but difficult for the people to accept. They had to learn and acknowledge that the God who led them out of Egypt was the only true God, and they could not serve as His people while worshipping other gods.

The people of Israel often struggled to remember the importance and benefits of obeying God's word, even though they made efforts to follow other commandments. However, God, being the true and living God, understood that if the people wholeheartedly obeyed the first commandment, it would lay a strong foundation for their obedience to the rest of the commandments. This initial commandment served as a cornerstone for the remaining ones. Once the foundation of obedience was firmly established in their hearts, it would make it easier for them to obey the subsequent commandments. Obedience, therefore, needed to be cultivated as a fundamental attitude of the heart right from the beginning.

The Bible extensively describes Israel's public worship, which encompassed offerings, verbal praises, musical instruments, prayers, and grand feasts. To gain a deeper understanding of the form and spirit in which godly Israel worshipped, one must turn to the pages of the Bible. It is within its contents that we can discover the remarkable manner in which Israel worshipped God in a way that honoured and pleased Him.

The children of Israel had a serious problem that prevented them from worshipping God faithfully. They took on the characteristics of idol worship and imitated the godless nations around them. When the Israelites came out of Egypt, they came from a land of many gods, where each god represented different aspects of their lives. Consequently, the people became confused in their worship. Although they knew the true and living God, they were serving and worshipping both the true God and idols at the same time, which was not acceptable. The two could not flourish in the same heart. Worshipping many gods to obtain maximum blessings was a common practice in Israel, but they were warned against it. Having no real commitment to God, they had their minds and hands in more than one fire at the same time. The people were warned about this action because God had plans for them if they worshipped the true and living God without adding other gods to the list. It was initially not difficult for them to obey when God told them to worship and believe in Him alone, but it eventually became a problem as they took on an attitude of disobedience against God.

MAKE GOD THE CENTRE

God should be the centre of worship for those who call on the name of the Lord Jesus Christ. True worship does not depend on the presence or use of things, geographical locations, or reliance on sight or touch. True worshippers exercise faith in God regardless of their surroundings, maintaining a worshipful attitude. Without this, they cannot be His people, no matter how faithfully they keep the other commandments. This is why God emphasised the first commandment more than the others, saying, *"You shall have no other gods before me"* (Exodus 20:2). By complying with this command in their hearts and choosing to serve Him, being justified by faith, sanctified, and standing in Jesus' name, without condemnation, they are transformed and their minds are renewed. Praise the Lord! It is necessary to exchange wrong attitudes for right behaviours and approach a holy God with the right attitude, even in the dark hours of midnight. An attitude of worship draws on memories of the past, reminding us how God came through in times of insecurity just before daylight. Before it gets worse, it gets better. God grants wisdom and perspective, knowing the best course of action. True wisdom comes from knowing and trusting God, and it goes beyond merely finding Him—it leads to greater understanding and sharing knowledge with others. The difficulty arises when people prioritise wealth, attraction, and success over wisdom. Although wisdom is a greater asset and strength, it often goes unnoticed by the masses. Wisdom is even more effective than material gain, but it is not often regarded, and wise people are often ignored.

Do you find yourself in the category of being too skeptical? Do you only see value in cheering for others or taking the leading role when you are involved? Instead of being quick to put others in their place with skepticism, why not enjoy the game and encourage others to shine? It is important to change that attitude and support those who come into your circle, allowing them to shine. Sometimes, no matter how much effort someone puts in, it is never enough for certain individuals to appreciate them until they are no longer around. Some are even ready to offer dead flowers that quickly fade away.

Jesus condemned the attitude of His generation because, regardless of what He said or did, they cynically and skeptically challenged Him. They held onto their comfortable, secure, and self-centred view of life, resisting any inconsistencies that listening to God might require them to change (see Matthew 15:8). It is important for us not to adopt a similar mindset and to learn from their negative example. This is also a way to cultivate the right kind of attitude to approach God.

Eight

The Selfish Attitude of a Man Swallowed by a Fish

An intriguing story is told in the Bible about a man named Jonah and his encounter with a large fish. Jonah was assigned a specific mission in a distant town, where the people needed to hear the gospel of salvation. Despite their resistance, it was crucial to deliver the message. However, Jonah displayed a negative attitude and boarded a ship heading in the opposite direction. He held objections towards both the people and the place, believing that the inhabitants were extremely wicked, unlikely to listen to him and did not deserve God's attention.

In the midst of his selfish disposition towards the people, a storm suddenly erupted one night while he was lodging in his cabin. God, determined to pursue Jonah, unleashed a mighty tempest at sea. As the wind rose, powerful waves crashed, demolishing everything in their path and shattering the ship into pieces. The roar of the tempest reminded Jonah of his duty—to go and deliver the message to the people. He realised that he could run, but he couldn't hide.

While the rest of the people on the ship were alarmed by the fierce tempest, Jonah remained unconcerned. The crew questioned him about the cause of the storm, sensing that something was amiss. They urged him to call on his God or prepare for death. After some time, they discovered Jonah sound asleep in the depths of the ship. Neither the noise nor any sense of guilt awakened him. They approached him again and roused him to pray. The darkness and fear overwhelmed him, leading him to panic and jump overboard. Miraculously, a great fish swallowed him, but he remained alive inside.

Inside the belly of the enormous fish, Jonah tumbled for three long days and nights. It was a dark and terrifying experience. Confronted by the consequences of his wrong attitude, he found himself in silence. However, he knew how to pray for help and relief from inside the fish. Despite his fear and shame, he continued praying until God's mercy reached him at the lowest point of his life. His pride was shattered into many pieces. This serves as a warning that disobedience can lead you down a path of despair.

In his distress, Jonah realised that he was about to be digested by the fish. His attitude hit rock bottom, prompting him to take positive action and call out to God for deliverance and God heard his cry. The Lord caused the fish to vomit Jonah out unharmed, with not a single bone broken. He likely had only a few bruises here and there. Despite his disobedience, the mission was still valid; God did not change His mind. Whether Jonah chose the easy or hard way, he had to go where God sent him. *"And we* know that in all things God works for the good of those who love him, who[a] have been called according to his purpose" (Romans 8:28).

This demonstrates how God's ears are always open to our cries, no matter where we are. Choosing to call on the name of the Lord is not just reserved for times of trouble but should be done at all times, as God's mercies endure forever.

Jonah learned a difficult lesson about doing things his own way and eventually submitted to God, doing what was right—obeying Him. Satan has never been able to destroy God's plans. God would rather break and reshape us to fulfill His will, even if we cannot see His hands at work, orchestrating everything. How merciful and caring is our God towards unruly creatures?

Our attitude naturally colours our personality. Although we cannot choose what happens to us, we can choose our attitude towards each situation. Therefore, the secret to a cheerful heart is to fill our minds with thoughts that are true, pure, and lovely—to dwell on the good things in life. Evaluate your attitude and be mindful of what you allow into your mind. Make rigorous changes, unafraid to root out anything that robs, steals, and destroys your faith in God. Some individuals with proud behaviour and attitudes pay little attention to their weaknesses. They believe they are above the frailties of common people..

Destructive prideful attitudes are prevalent among individuals, who behave selfishly and express a self-centred mindset. Unfortunately, a prideful attitude often tarnishes one's character and blinds them to what is happening around them. Those with a selfish attitude seldom concern themselves with the welfare of others until something drastic occurs. However, their state of mind can easily trip them up. Often, proud people fail to realise that pride can lead to a unpleasant fall if they continue on until it is too late

SELFISH ATTITUDES TOWARDS OTHERS

Here is another example from 1 Samuel 28. When Samuel served as a judge in Israel, he faithfully obeyed God and carried out his leadership responsibilities for years. However, the people considered him unfit for service, claiming that he was too old to judge Israel as he did in his younger years. During Samuel's rule as judge, an elder approached him at his house with a problem. The people refused to obey Samuel's voice and requested a king to rule over them. In short, they criticised Samuel for being old, and his sons did not walk in his ways.

Samuel was indeed old, and his experience should have been an advantage in ruling as a judge. It was also true that his sons displayed a wrong attitude by not following in their father's footsteps. Directing their request to Samuel, the people desired a king who would exude external pomp and power, just like the rulers of other nations. The people's plea for a king was not a rebellion against Samuel's leadership, which was commendable. However, it was still an evil proposal. Many men who performed well in a state of subjection were corrupted by preferment and power. Honour often changes people's minds, and more often than not, it leads to negative outcomes.

The manner and approach of the people displeased God. Samuel, exhausted by his public responsibilities, expected his strength and spirit to be recognised. He had recommended his sons for their duties and commission, but unfortunately, they did not follow his ways. Their character was the opposite of their father's, rendering them unfit for the entrusted positions. Despite this, Samuel's sons were appointed as judges and settled far away from him.

While Samuel still wore his mantle and appeared unimpressive in the people's eyes, they envisioned a king dressed in purple robes, surrounded by guards and exhibiting grandeur. Samuel felt deeply hurt by the people's selfish attitude when they requested a king to judge them.

This selfish attitude of the people drove Samuel to his knees. He didn't respond immediately or provide an answer but instead prayed to the Lord for guidance. Whenever we face adversity, it is essential to pray for direction—where, how, when, and what practical actions to take. God provided Samuel with instructions, assuring him that he should not consider it strange or be displeased. The rejection was not directed at Samuel personally; rather, it was a rejection of God. If God allows Himself to be subjected to indignities, we should maintain a right attitude and patiently endure them. God instructed Samuel to heed the people's voice—they were to have a king. However, God also revealed that this decision would lead to consequences and the people would experience the difference between His governance and that of a king. God knew the people's hearts. If they were not satisfied, they would likely rebel against Samuel, abandon their religious practices, and turn to the gods of other nations.

The people's wrong attitude towards Samuel stemmed from their perception of him as an old man who should retire from ruling over them. Samuel reminded the people of everything God had said and pointed out that it was not himself they had rejected, but God. He presented the idea of having a king to the people, asking them to be mindful of the type of rule they would now have to live under. The king would have a retinue of attendants, and the people's sons would be appointed to serve him, tending to his grounds and reaping his harvest. The king would maintain a great table, have a standing army for guards and garrisons, and possess favoured individuals who would enrich his inheritance with great revenues and power. Moreover, the king would claim one-tenth of the fruits of their land and cattle. However, the people obstinately demanded a king, stating, *"We will have a king over us"* (1 Samuel 28:5).

The people were deaf to reason and oblivious to their own interests. Regardless of what God or Samuel said, the people insisted on having a king, even if it brought inconvenience upon them and their children. Samuel brought the people's negative attitude to the Lord's attention. God graciously listened to Samuel's report on the people's concerns, just as friends whisper to one another. Finally, God instructed Samuel to grant the people a king since they were so determined. God said, "Give them a king and let them make the most of it" (v22). Thus, God allowed the people to have what they desired, even though it might not be to their advantage.

ISRAEL'S ISSUE

The problem with the people of Israel is that they lacked the attitude of humility and reverence required to trust in God's wisdom concerning what was best for their lives. A person with a positive attitude will proclaim the greatness of God, even when they may not experience it at the time. When our actions are negative, God is still willing to forgive. When we are weak, He provides strength. When we are lost, He shows us the way. When we feel afraid, He offers courage. When we stumble, His hands steady our steps. When we are broken, He is ready to mend us and restore us. These are the benefits of remaining humble and maintaining a positive attitude towards God's will for our lives. God grants us the desires, abilities, conditions, and right connections to become all that we were meant to be. He assures us to stay positive on our journey. If we veer off the right path, He will guide us back, for those who desire to know the way. As it is *written, "Whether you turn to the right or to the left, your ears will hear a voice behind you saying, 'This is the way, walk in it'"* (Isaiah 30:21). Philippians 2:13 also tells us, *"...for it is God who works in you to will and to act in order to fulfill his good purpose."*

Therefore, the Holy One of Israel says, *"Because you have rejected this message, relied on oppression, and depended on deceit, sin will become like a high wall—cracked, bulging, and suddenly collapsing, breaking into pieces like shattered pottery. Among its fragments, not a fragment will be found for taking coals from a hearth or scooping water out of a cistern"* (Isaiah 30:4-5).

When you find yourself unsure of which direction to take, trust in God's guidance and watchful care, as stated in Psalms 32:8.

He promises to instruct and teach you in the way you should go, counselling and watching over you. However, God warns against being stubborn and unyielding like horses or mules that require bits and bridles to be controlled. Instead, allow yourself to be guided by God's wisdom and love, which can transform your attitude and purpose without the need for punishment.

God is the ultimate giver, exemplified by His sacrificial gift of His Son, Jesus, to redeem humanity even when they were His enemies. Jesus, the sacrificial Lamb, took upon Himself the sins of the world, exchanging them for His righteousness. This act of atonement demonstrates God's immeasurable love and kindness. Trusting in Christ allows you to receive His righteousness and be grateful for His mercy and grace (2 Corinthians 5:21).

Jesus consistently exhibited complete dedication to God. For instance, when Jesus and His parents went on a day trip, He remained in the temple, engrossed in His Father's business. His love-driven attitude serves as an example for us to love one another and imitate His excellent qualities, which are produced by the Holy Spirit. An attitude of peace, joy, patience, kindness, faithfulness, gentleness, and positive thinking can make a significant difference in your life and the lives of those around you.

DON'T LET NEGATIVE ATTITUDES PREVAIL

Unfortunately, negative attitudes are prevalent in society, even throughout biblical history. It is regrettable to see how these negative attitudes can lead people astray and make them feel hopeless and discouraged. It is essential to remember what God has done in the past, especially in times of blessing and abundance. Acknowledge that everything comes from God, and stay positive even when others may view your situation negatively. Trust in Him, and you will succeed.

Reminding ourselves of all that God has done for us protects us against developing a selfish attitude. Moses reminded the people to follow God's commands and not forget His faithfulness in leading them through the wilderness for forty years. God used the wilderness as a school to humble and test the people's hearts, teaching them to rely on His commands and discipline. Similarly, when Satan tempted Jesus with wrong attitudes during His wilderness experience, Jesus stood firm, reminding Satan of what is written in God's word. He did not give in to His immediate desires.

Eating food to satisfy one's hunger is not inherently wrong. It is the context in which it occurs that can determine its rightness or wrongness. In the case of Jesus, the devil's timing was inappropriate, as Jesus was in the desert to fast, not to eat. Jesus deliberately chose to relinquish His divine ability to use unlimited power independently in order to experience humility. He refused to employ His power to transform stones into bread.

There is much to learn from how Jesus resisted the temptation to fulfill His immediate physical need for bread, despite being naturally hungry. In the same way, every child of God should resist the temptation to engage in behaviours that God forbids, such as engaging in sexual activities before marriage or repay evil to a person who has hurt you. Indulging in such behaviours only serves to gratify evil desires and does not bring true satisfaction or promote a right attitude. It is important to remember that as new creatures in Christ, we have been given an understanding of the principles of righteousness and should strive to do what is right.

Jesus' sacrificial death on the cross has fulfilled God's wrath for human sin, and there is no longer a need for sacrifices. Through His death and resurrection, believers are made perfect in God's sight. However, spiritual discipline and daily guidance are still necessary for growth and transformation. It is crucial to have the right attitude and not take God's blessings for granted, but rather be thankful for everything and manage them in accordance with His will.

Friends, endeavour to cultivate a positive and humble attitude, allowing God to guide your life and transform your character. Remember His love and sacrifice, imitate Christ's qualities, and appreciate His blessings. Stay steadfast in times of testing, and remain grateful for God's discipline and guidance. You will then be able to insulate yourself against a selfish attitude.

nine

The Attitude of Worshipping with Musical Instruments

The attitude of worshipping God, including the use of musical instruments, serves an important role in Israel's worship and celebration. Musical instruments are not only used to accompany vocalists but also to enhance the singing itself. When the people were delivered from great danger, they sang with joy and offered praises to God. In our present world, Psalms and hymns are great ways to express release of praises and thanksgiving, especially after going through troubles (Exodus 15:1).

An example of this is the song of Moses, which is the oldest recorded song in the world and an epic poem celebrating God's victory. It lifted the hearts and voices of the people outwardly and upwardly. Singing is an expression of love and gratitude and a creative way to worship, passing down as an oral tradition. Christians are encouraged to speak to one another with "*... psalms, hymns, and spiritual songs, singing and making music in your heart to the Lord, always giving thanks to God the Father* *for everything in the name of the Lord Jesus Christ"* (Ephesians 5:19-20).

The excellent use of music is a gift that allows us to render praise and thanksgiving to God and express our emotions, sorrows, and joys. The addition of music in worship is not inappropriate in itself; music was created by God. Worshipping with music can enhance our praises to God as long as the use of music has a positive impact on our relationship with Him. The music industry is vast and effective in various contexts such as funeral services, social entertainments, processions, weddings, dedications, and even as a positive influence during times of mental disorder or sorrow. The sound of music can be helpful in lifting spirits and providing comfort.

David, as a young man, wrote many songs and was hired to play the harp for King Saul during his challenging times. Many of David's songs can be found in the book of Psalms. Psalm 8, written as a holiday hymn, invites us to *"Sing for the joy of the Lord God your strength; shout aloud to the God of Jacob!"* David, a talented musician, played his harp and brought music into the temple. He wrote inspiring Psalms and lamentations, including one in memory of Saul and his son Jonathan, David's closest friend. Despite Saul causing trouble for David, he composed lamenting music that showed empathy towards the king and his son. Instead of harbouring hatred and resentment, David chose to focus on the good that Saul had done.

Let the music begin! Strike the tambourine, play the melodious harp and lyre. Some may even dance before the Lord, but this is only allowed when the attitude is right, both towards God and one another. David established music in temple worship services, choosing song leaders and choirs to perform regularly in the temple.

During the days of the Old Testament, worship services were designed to engage all five senses, serving to deepen the significance of religious ceremonies. Each sense played a role in the worship experience. For instance, the eyes were captivated by the beauty of the tabernacle, adorned with meaningful colours and intricate designs. Through sight, worshippers could appreciate the visual representation of their faith.

Listening with the ears was also a crucial aspect of worship, as it allowed people to celebrate the Creator's handiwork by discerning the subtle nuances of sound. The melodies, readings, and prayers offered during worship services resonated with worshippers, evoking emotions and fostering a deeper connection to their spiritual practices.

Touch was incorporated in worship through symbolic gestures. For instance, laying hands on the heads of animals designated for sacrifice symbolised the individual's placement and identification with the act of offering. This physical touch added a tangible element to the worship experience.

The sense of smell was engaged through the aroma of burnt sacrifices. The familiar scent served as a sensory reminder of the offerings presented to God, signifying devotion and surrender.

Lastly, the sense of taste played a role in worship during celebratory feasts and offerings. Partaking in specific foods and meals held symbolic significance, allowing for the memorisation and reinforcement of important scriptural teachings and events. By involving all five senses, worship in the Old Testament sought to create a comprehensive and immersive experience, reinforcing the religious rituals and deepening the connection between worshippers and their faith.

Through skillful playing or listening to music, we can reflect on our spiritual needs, limitations, and celebrate the goodness of God towards us. Music and worship go hand in hand, and worshippers should involve their whole being because music helps lift a person's well-being to a higher level in the presence of God.

IN HARMONY

Worshipping in harmony with musical instruments involves a combination of musical notes that are pleasant and attractive. It is an effective way to give glory to God and is beneficial to worshippers because it speaks to a deeper part of who we are. The principle of harmony should touch every aspect of singing, preaching, and the use of spiritual gifts. Those who contribute to the worship service, such as singers, speakers, and readers, must exercise genuine love towards God and others, blending harmony like a chief motivational speaker using words in ways that strengthen the faith of the hearers. It is vital that church services be conducted in an orderly manner, encouraging and provoking other worshippers to forget about themselves and enjoy the fulfillment of worshipping God with musical instruments. Preparation and practice are necessary for worship to become a personal lifestyle that invites others to experience it as well. Otherwise, chaos and mistrust can arise. You cannot worship God in your own strength or without inviting the Holy Spirit to guide you through your worship. The Holy Spirit knows the Father better than you do. The Father is looking for true worshippers, who offer their praise with thanksgiving, prayer, meditation, and understanding, for these act as powerful armour on the part of the worshipper (see John 4:23). These principles will enhance your Christian living and help you better understand and overcome pitfalls that might hinder your path.

Cooperative prayer serves as a crucial foundation before engaging in any act of worship. By coming together in prayer, individuals can align their hearts and minds with the Word of God, seeking His guidance and wisdom. It is through prayer that one can clear the path of confusion and obstacles that may hinder the plans of the enemy.

Cooperative prayer involves joining together with others in a unified purpose, lifting up prayers, supplications, and praises to God. This collective act of seeking God's presence and direction creates a supportive and empowering atmosphere for worship.

The theme of worship is beautifully expressed throughout the Psalms, where individuals find joy and receive both material and spiritual blessings, prompting them to offer thanks and praise to God. However, there are those who, due to broken relationships or other reasons, may struggle to fully grasp the essence of true worship. This can create a division among worshippers, with some actively engaged in true worship while others remain on the sidelines.

In such situations, it is important to encourage and help those individuals reconnect with the active flow of the Holy Spirit. They may need to seek forgiveness and renew their relationship with God in order to regain confidence and experience the depth of worship. God values obedience and persistence, and by seeking His approval, individuals can cultivate the right attitude of worship and praise.

The Psalms depict the beauty of unity and harmony among believers. When brothers and sisters dwell together in harmony, it is likened to precious oil poured on the head, running down Aaron's beard and robes. It is comparable to the refreshing dew of Mount Hermon descending upon Mount Zion. In such an environment, the Lord bestows His blessings, including abundant and everlasting life. The Psalms declare, *"Behold, how good and how pleasant it is For brethren to dwell together in unity! It is like the precious oil upon the head, running down on the beard, the beard of Aaron, running down on the edge of his garments. It is like the dew of Hermon, descending upon the mountains of Zion; for there the LORD commanded the blessing— life forevermore"* (Psalm 133:1-2 NKJV).

Therefore, it is crucial for believers to cultivate unity, forgiveness, and a genuine desire for harmonious relationships within the community of worshippers. This creates an atmosphere where the blessings of God flow freely and worship becomes a powerful and transformative experience for all involved.

When we worship with musical instruments, the rhythm is what makes the total difference in music. Various instruments were used to create this effect when praising the Lord, including trumpets, lutes, harps, tambourines, dances, string instruments, and flutes. Praising God with loud cymbals is mentioned as well: *"Let everything that has breath praise the Lord"* (Psalm 150:6). By developing a reverential attitude, perfect harmony is inspired and established in a worshipful attitude that brings glory to God. Worship should be a bowing down of the heart, soul, and spirit to the Father, Son, and Holy Spirit. It is a time of awe (see Psalms 137:3-6).

Where you worship God does not matter. For instance, in Christ's discourse with the woman at the well, He said, "The hour is coming, and now is, when the true worshipers will worship the Father in spirit and truth." Christ emphasised the importance of conscience and put little emphasis on the physical place of worship. True worshippers are not bound to a specific location; they can worship God everywhere and anywhere, as long as they worship in spirit and truth.

WORSHIPPING GOD WITH OUR INSTRUMENTS
THE TRUMPET

The trumpet is a metal wind instrument with a narrow tube that widens near the end. In the Bible, the trumpet was used as a significant instrument in worship. It had various purposes, including warning of judgment, calling the forces of good and evil to battle, and announcing the return of the Messiah.

Trumpets were included among the musical instruments in the temple, and they were used effectively as a mighty force at the falling of Jericho's walls. However, Jesus cautioned against using trumpets to attract attention to one's acts of charity, emphasising, again, the importance of genuine and humble worship.

In biblical times, the priests and Levites were the identified chief trumpeters, although it is possible that non-priests also played the instrument. The trumpet was used in various occasions, such as the inauguration of Solomon's temple, where 120 trumpets were played. Imagine that wonderful sound as the trumpeters praised God, knowing that He had accepted the sons of Aaron.

The trumpet serves as a symbol of warning, urging believers to ensure their faith is firmly fixed in God. It signifies the certainty of judgment and calls for a genuine and sincere worship of God.

VOICES IN SINGING

Singing is a beautiful way to express gratitude and thanksgiving to the Lord. It is a means of worship that inspires the mind and brings it into the right attitude. Singing spiritual songs without the use of instruments can elevate the spirit and lead to a higher level of praise.

Many individuals are gifted with beautiful voices, and although training may be necessary, the voice plays a vital part in worship. Singing has been practiced throughout history, and it is mentioned in the Bible as a form of worship. King David, for example, was a talented musician who played the harp and used music to worship God in the temple. He composed many Psalms, expressing his praises and thanksgiving to God, so we can comfortably consider David a singer.

When David found himself pursued by his enemies seeking his life, he used singing as a means to draw strength and protection from the Lord. David wrote in Psalm 59:16-17, *"But I will sing of your strength; I will sing aloud of your steadfast love in the morning. For you have been to me a fortress and a refuge in the day of my distress. O my Strength, I will sing praises to you, for you, O God, are my fortress, the God who shows me steadfast love."* He expressed his trust in God's power and mercy through songs of praise, acknowledging Him as his defender and refuge in times of trouble. David understood that singing was not merely an act of musical expression, but a powerful means to connect with God and receive His protection.

Throughout the Bible, there are numerous examples of how singing helped God's people endure difficult times. Even in the darkest moments, God grants His people a song that brings comfort and joy. Singing becomes a way to declare and make known God's attributes and deeds to all generations. It serves as a reminder of His deliverance and a refuge in times of trouble. The melodies of these songs resonate with the righteousness of God and provide solace for the sorrowful. In Isaiah 30:29, it is mentioned, *"And you will sing as on the night you celebrate a holy festival; your hearts will rejoice as when people playing pipes go up to the mountain of the LORD, to the Rock of Israel."*

In Psalm 89:1-2, the psalmist declares, *"I will sing of the LORD's great love forever; with my mouth I will make your faithfulness known through all generations. I will declare that your love stands firm forever, that you have established your faithfulness in heaven itself."*

Singing melodious songs of God's righteousness is mentioned in Psalm 71:22, where it says, *"I will praise you with the harp for your faithfulness, my God; I will sing praise to you with the lyre, Holy One of Israel."*

In Psalm 137:1-3, the psalmist expresses the sorrow of the Israelites in exile, saying, *"By the waters of Babylon, there we sat down and wept when we remembered Zion. On the willows there we hung up our lyres. For there our captors required of us songs, and our tormentors, mirth, saying, 'Sing us one of the songs of Zion!'"* (NKJV)

These verses highlight the significance of singing in worship and in times of distress. Singing allows believers to express their trust in God, proclaim His faithfulness, and find solace and strength in His presence. It is a powerful way to connect with God and declare His praises. No wonder believers are encouraged to engage in singing, using psalms, hymns, and spiritual songs to make melody in their hearts to the Lord.

THE CYMBALS

In biblical times, cymbals were percussion instruments used to accompany other instruments in worship. They were made of copper and had different effects, including a melodious sound and a clashing sound. The clashing sound of the cymbals is compared to the speaking of tongues, emphasising the importance of love and intentionality in worship over loud noise devoid of meaning. *'If I speak in the tongues of men or of angels, but do not have love, I am only a resounding gong or a clanging cymbal"* (1 Corinthians 13:1).

THE FLUTE

The flute was a popular musical instrument in New Testament times. It was played at joyous occasions, banquets, weddings, and even in times of sadness. Flutes were often played during mourning, accompanied by professional mourners. In a Middle Eastern custom, these mourners were often hired to create a noisy atmosphere during funeral processions, and minstrels, including flutists, were part of this practice.

In the account of Jesus raising a young girl from the dead, He made the statement that she was not dead but sleeping. This indicates that her death would be temporary, as Jesus had the power to bring her back to life. When Jesus arrived at the house of the girl's family and saw the people mourning and playing flutes, He asked them to leave. He then went inside, took the girl by the hand, and she was raised back to life. This miraculous event demonstrated Jesus' authority over death and His ability to bring life even in the face of mourning and despair.

In certain situations, flutes were used by the prophets, as seen when Samuel anointed Saul, and a procession of prophets came down from the hill with musical instruments.

THE HARP

The harp, also known as the lyre, is one of the oldest stringed instruments mentioned in Scripture. It was used in temple orchestras, and certain Levites were appointed to give continual praise and thanks to God. The harp is associated with King

David, who was an accomplished harpist and frequently spoke about music in the Psalms. He praised the Lord with the harp, making music on the ten-stringed lyre and sang a new song to the Lord.

In the Bible, Jabel is described as the father of those who play the harp and flute. He is mentioned in the genealogy of Cain in Genesis 4:21. This indicates that he was associated with the development of musical instruments, particularly the harp and flute.

During the period when the Israelites were taken captive in Babylon, they experienced great sadness and longing for their homeland. As a result, they had no desire to play their musical instruments, including the harp. They symbolically hung their harps on the willow trees, a gesture that expressed their grief and loss (Psalm 137:2). This event reflects the emotional state of the Israelites during their exile. The psalmist laments the loss of Jerusalem and expresses the inability to sing the songs of Zion in a foreign land. The image of hanging their harps on the willow trees signifies their sorrow and their inability to find joy or engage in music in such a distressing situation.

THE PSALTERY

The psaltery is a musical instrument that was part of the temple orchestra. It was used in government services and proclamations. In Babylonian religious culture, psalteries were frequently played during important events, such as when King Nebuchadnezzar erected a large statue and commanded all people to bow down and worship it. Daniel and his friends refused to worship the statue, even though it led to their condemnation.

THE TAMBOURINE

The tambourine, along with the cymbals, was used in Israel's worship. Miriam, Moses' sister, was skilled in playing the tambourine, and she led the women in singing and dancing after the crossing of the Red Sea. Scripture records her words as she sang, *"Miriam sang to them: 'Sing to the Lord, for he is highly exalted. Both horse and driver he has hurled into the sea'"* (Exodus 15:21). The tambourine was used to celebrate and praise God for His deliverance. However, Isaiah also mentioned how people would indulge in drinking and partying, having musical instruments at their banquets, but not having regard for the deeds of the Lord.

Overall, these various musical instruments were used in worship to express praise, gratitude, and devotion to God. They played an important role in biblical times and continue to be used in worship today, allowing believers to engage their hearts, minds, and voices in praising God.

THE USE OF THE HORN IN WORSHIP

Worshipping God with the horn has been practiced on various occasions in biblical history. For example, when King David brought up the covenant of the Lord, a grand musical procession was organised to accomplish the worship ceremony. The sounding of the horn was intended to heighten excitement and elevate the hearts and minds of the people, creating a memorable moment.

The horn had several uses, such as blowing it to assemble the forces of Israel or sounding an alarm against a city to be attacked. It served as a means of directing movements and signaling others during military operations. When there was an enemy attack, the horn would give warning and alert the people.

The horn was not only a musical wind instrument but also a signaling instrument. It didn't have a separate mouthpiece for blowing, and its sound would alert the people when trouble from the enemy was near. In one instance, when Gideon's small army could not win a battle in their own strength, the blowing of the horn signaled others in their camp to join the fight.

The use of the horn demonstrated that victory did not depend on their own strength or numbers but on their obedience and commitment to God. When the enemy heard the sound of the horn surrounding the camp, they would flee in fear. This showed that victory came from God and not from their own abilities.

For example, Gideon commanded three hundred people to blow their horns, causing the whole enemy camp to be thrown into confusion. Everyone sounded their horns and shouted, "A sword for the Lord and for Gideon!" (Judges 7:20) he blowing of the horn also had other uses, such as announcing the new moon and proclaiming the year of Jubilee. It added to the joyful spirit of various occasions.

In the context of worshipping God, the horn was also used by the priests who would take the lead in blowing this instrument when marching around Jericho's walls (Judges 7:15).

WORSHIPPING WITH A COMPLETE MUSICAL ORCHESTRA

Worshipping with a complete musical orchestra, led by the Holy Spirit, is a powerful combination. When believers come together in harmony, lifting their voices and using string instruments to express joyful praises, it can have a mighty impact. The Holy Spirit's presence and anointing during worship can bring about exceptional effects and edify the believers.

While musical instruments enhance the act of worshipping Jehovah God, it is important to note that David, who played musical instruments under the anointing of the Holy Spirit, never solely relied on the sound of the instruments for satisfaction. Instruments are made by human hands and should not be the sole priority in worshipping God. If instruments are not available, believers can still blend their voices in one accord and cultivate melodious praise to the Lord. The right attitude and an obedient heart are crucial in worshipping God, regardless of the presence or absence of musical accompaniment.

Worship leaders have a responsibility in this awesome task of arranging and leading worship. They should lead with integrity, seeking the Holy Spirit's anointing for clear direction and avoiding chaos or confusion. It is important for worship leaders to have a personal experience of worshipping God and to develop an attitude of thanksgiving as an integral part of praise. No instrument or tool can substitute or accomplish its purpose without the greater power of God. When a tool boasts of greater power than the one who uses it, it is in danger of being discarded. We are useful to the extent that we allow God to use us.

Ten

Attitudes Towards Prayer and Homage

Praying is like having a two-way communication with God. You pray, and God answers through His Word. Prayer is a connection to God our Father through the name of Jesus. All things are possible when we pray and believe, for God hears us. Men ought to pray and not faint, praying without ceasing. God is a rewarder of those who diligently seek Him. Your prayers should be with understanding and expectation in faith, believing that God is faithful to all His promises. As you engage in prayer, release your cares and fears to your heavenly Father, and let the Holy Spirit help you in prayer. He will uphold you.

There are many instances where Jesus prayed publicly and also engaged in private prayers. Jesus recommended private prayers and condemned ostentatious and long prayers done for pretense.

An excellent practice and attitude in prayer is to pay homage to God. This practice was observed by the Pharisees and Scribes, although some Scribes had fallen into hypocrisy. Christians have adopted many customs and practices from the Jewish synagogue, and these practices were not disapproved by God. In the Christian Greek scriptures, the same attitudes and gestures of prayer are mentioned, but they do not support the idea of assuming piety and sanctimoniousness through facial or bodily expressions. The posture is not essential; what matters is coming to God through His Son Jesus with a clean and sincere attitude. Just as the hymn says, we come to God without a plea of our own, but just as we are, meaning in sincerity. Many people from different backgrounds and cultures have sought to reach God in prayer, and the important thing is to approach Him with honesty and sincerity.

Another essential aspect of prayer is having clean hands and a pure heart, which God will never turn away. God's attitude towards your prayers is founded in Christ, showing the heart of God the Father and what He thinks about His children. God is not selfish, begrudging, or stingy. Therefore, there is no need to beg or grovel when approaching Him. God, as a loving Father, understands your cares, and the Holy Spirit helps you in prayer. Think of the kindness of God towards you, just as your parents and friends are kind.

When you approach God in prayer and worship, your attitude should not be casual but reverential, as though you were approaching an earthly king to make a request. Queen Esther's approach to the king, risking her life for the Jewish people, serves as an example. In God's economy of favour, you can come boldly to the throne of grace without a middle wall between you and Him. Through Jesus' death on the cross, the middle wall of partition was removed to redeem mankind from their sins. Approach God in the right attitude and let go of wrong attitudes.

The position in prayer is of least concern. What is most important is that the individual prays with a clean heart to God, the hearer of prayers. God is a prayer-hearing God who listens to prayers from the heart, regardless of the specific physical position. You must have an attitude of forgiveness towards others so that your Father may forgive your sins. While at prayer, remember to pray for others, especially those who have wronged you. Let go of grudges and pray with selfless motives, seeking the good of God's kingdom and others. You may choose to pray while taking a walk, waiting for a bus, standing in line, or doing household chores. Take every opportunity to connect with God in prayer from the heart. If an event or activity is important, you will schedule it for a specific day and time. Likewise, prioritise your time for prayer and the building up of the kingdom of God in these last days.

Prayer is not only about presenting our personal requests to God, but it is also a powerful act of interceding for others. Just as Jesus intercedes for us before the Father, we are called to pray for others and bring their concerns before God. Your prayer requests should be centred on the well-being of God's kingdom and others, rather than being driven by personal interests and desires. Though it may be tempting to ask for personal gain and instant fulfillment, take note that Jesus, in His own prayers, had the interest of His Father's will in mind. So, the next time you pray, express your needs and desires to God, but also ask for His will to be done in your life.

SHOWING HOMAGE

The Bible records numerous examples of individuals approaching God in prayer with homage. One such example is found in the life of Ezra. Ezra praised God for all that He had done for him and showed deep reverence and honour towards God throughout his life. In turn, God chose to honour Ezra and used him to accomplish great things.

Ezra's reverence for God was evident in his commitment to studying and faithfully applying God's word. He took the Scriptures seriously and sought to align his actions and life with God's commands. This devotion to God's word allowed Ezra to gain wisdom and insight, which he then shared with others. He became a great teacher and model of sharing the Word of God, impacting the lives of many.

Ezra's example teaches us the importance of honouring God in our prayers and lives. By studying and applying God's word, we can grow in wisdom and understanding. This, in turn, enables us to have a positive influence on others as we share the truths we have learned. Ultimately, approaching God with homage and reverence sets us on the right path and opens doors for God's blessings and guidance in our lives.

Like Ezra, Daniel exemplified unwavering dedication in paying homage through his commitment to prayer. Even when the law prohibited praying to any god other than the king, Daniel did not hide his prayer habits. He continued to pray three times a day, openly defying the new law despite knowing that his enemies in the government were aware of his disobedience. Daniel's steadfast devotion to prayer showcased his deep reliance on

God's strength and guidance, especially in the face of difficult tasks and challenges. His unwavering commitment serves as an inspiring example of one who remained faithful and dedicated in paying homage to God through consistent prayer.

PRAYING TO THE RIGHT GOD

In matters of worship, it is important to discern between those who pray to the God they believe in and those who pray to the true and living God. Job, in his wisdom, warned against the danger of being enticed by objects of reverence, such as the sun or moon, and engaging in gestures or acts of worship towards them. These actions can divert one's heart from the worship of the true God.

There are individuals who, in their faith, confess their prayers to figures like the Virgin Mary, considering her as an intercessor, or they may worship other objects or deities, including animals, sun gods, moon gods, or anything they hold in higher regard than the true and living God. However, it is important to note that worshipping anything or anyone other than the true God goes against the teachings of the Bible.

Prayer is a matter of personal choice regarding who one offers prayers to and on behalf of. However, the fact remains that God desires true worship and warns against worshipping anything false. The Scriptures emphasise the exclusivity of worshipping the one true God, who has revealed Himself through His Son Jesus Christ. Jesus Himself proclaimed, *"I am the way, and the truth, and the life. No one comes to the Father except through me"* (John 14:6). Christians are called to worship and pray to the true and living God, seeking a personal relationship with Him through Jesus Christ, who is the mediator between God and humanity.

There are severe penalties for indulging in wrong behaviours and worshipping false gods, although some people continue to do so. For instance, devout Jews used to perform ceremonial hand and arm washing before each meal, believing it would cleanse them from any contact with unclean things they may have encountered, like in the marketplace. They also observed other traditions, such as washing cups, pitchers, and kettles. Jesus, however, pointed out that their thinking was flawed, and their worship was not motivated by love. Instead, they desired personal gain and sought to appear holy to increase their status. In reality, they became hypocrites, focusing more on reputation and outward appearance while keeping their hearts distant from God. It is important to be cautious and take heed of such attitudes.

BOWING DOWN IN PRAYER

The act of bowing down in prayer is mentioned in the Bible and has been a gesture of respect and reverence in various cultures and religions. In Hebrew religion, there was no set form of posture for prayer, but all assumed attitudes were highly respectful. Bowing down in prayer symbolised acknowledgement and respect for God's authority and sovereignty.

The Psalmist invites individuals to come and bow down in worship, kneeling before the Lord their Maker. Bowing down was a customary gesture of respect when greeting others or approaching matters of business. It demonstrated humility and submission before God.

In times of defeat or seeking mercy, the defeated would appear before their conqueror wearing sackcloth and ropes on their heads, symbolising captivity and submission. This act of bowing down signified their acknowledgement of their position and their plea for mercy.

Bowing down and showing respect were also customary among the Jewish community. For example, King Solomon, despite his royal position, showed respect to his mother by bowing down to her (see 1 Kings 2:19). This act of bowing was in accordance with the fifth commandment, which instructs children to honour their parents.

However, it is important to note that bowing down in prayer should be directed towards the true and living God. In the context of false worship, people would bow down to idols and even kiss them, as mentioned in 1 Kings 19:18. This kind of worship is not in alignment with the teachings of the Bible, as it involves the worship of false gods or objects.

The posture of bowing down in prayer can serve as a physical expression of reverence and submission to God. It is a way of humbling ourselves before Him and acknowledging His authority and greatness. However, it is crucial to remember that the posture itself is not the essence of prayer. What truly matters is the attitude of the heart and the sincerity of our connection with God.

STANDING IN PRAYER

Religious gestures and postures are observed in various forms of worship across different faiths. In Israel, for example, people stand at the Wailing Wall, also known as the Western Wall, to offer up prayers to God. Standing in prayer can symbolise a posture of attentiveness, reverence, and readiness to communicate with the divine.

In the Bible, there are instances where standing in prayer is mentioned. After Jesus' baptism, He was standing when He prayed, and it was at that moment that the heavens opened up, and the Holy Spirit descended upon Him in the form of a dove (Luke 3:21-22). This event marked the beginning of Jesus' public ministry and the confirmation of His divine mission.

While standing in prayer can be a significant posture, it is essential to remember that the physical position itself is not the primary focus of prayer. Instead, it is the condition of the heart and the sincerity of our connection with God that truly matter. Whether we stand, kneel, bow down, or adopt any other posture, the key is to approach God with humility, reverence, and a genuine desire to commune with Him.

In the Gospel of Luke, Jesus shares a parable about a Pharisee and a tax collector who went up to the temple to pray. The Pharisee stood and prayed, thanking God that he was not like other sinful people, while the tax collector stood at a distance, humbly beating his chest and asking God for mercy (Luke 18:9-14). In this parable, the act of standing in prayer is mentioned as a characteristic of the Pharisee's posture.

This example highlights the importance of the heart's condition and attitude during prayer rather than the specific physical posture. While standing in prayer can indicate a posture of confidence or self-righteousness, as seen in the Pharisee's case, it serves as a reminder that true prayer should be accompanied by humility, genuine repentance, and a recognition of our need for God's mercy.

KNEELING IN PRAYER

Kneeling in prayer is a common posture that signifies submission to the higher power of Almighty God. Jesus Himself knelt in the garden of Gethsemane, a stone's throw away from His disciples, and prayed, saying, *"Father, if it is Your will, remove this cup from Me; nevertheless, not My will, but Yours, be done"* (Luke 22:42).

Jesus set a positive example for His followers by kneeling in prayer to His heavenly Father. He knew the agony and horror He would face in the crucifixion and the complete separation from God the Father. Kneeling represents deep humility, and Jesus was not trying to avoid His mission of going to the cross when He expressed His feelings to His Father. It is never wrong to express your feelings to God. Jesus shared His dread of the upcoming trials while reaffirming His commitment to doing God's will. The torturous process was necessary for Jesus to die for the sins of the entire world.

Some individuals may be unable to kneel in prayer due to certain health issues or other hindering factors such as age or weight. While kneeling in prayer may sometimes be uncomfortable, it should not hinder a consistent prayer life. Although you cannot spend all your time on your knees, it is possible to gradually develop consistent prayer habits and cultivate the right attitude towards others, acknowledging your dependency on God in all circumstances.

At the time of Solomon's inauguration of the temple, he knelt in prayer. Solomon made a bronze scaffold and stood, bending his knees before the whole assembly of Israel, spreading forth his hands towards heaven. *"LORD, the God of Israel, there is no God like you in heaven above or on earth below—you who keep your covenant of love with your servants who continue wholeheartedly in your way. You have kept your promise to your servant David my father; with your mouth you have promised and with your hand you have fulfilled it—as it is today"* (1 Kings 8:23-24).

In Solomon's prayer representing the nation of Israel, he knelt at the inauguration of the temple, in a position with his hands spread up to heaven. When Solomon had finished praying and making supplication to the Lord, he arose from before the altar of the Lord and blessed the congregation (1 Kings 8:54).

In kneeling as he paid homage to the Lord, Solomon did not appoint a priest or prophets to do honours in prayer. Rather, he did it himself in the presence of all the congregation of Israel, reverencing in prayer and knowing how to express himself to God in a spiritual manner. His posture was very reverent and expressed humility. He was not shy in his request. Solomon spread forth his hands as if praying from an open, enlarged heart and presented them to heaven, expecting to receive from God what he prayed for. Solomon, with the right attitude in his dedicated prayer, marvelled as he said, *"But will God really dwell on earth? The heavens, even the highest heaven, cannot contain you. How much less this temple I have built!"* (1 Kings 8:22)

It was unusual for a king to kneel in front of the people he governed because kneeling meant submitting to higher authority. Solomon demonstrated great love and respect for God by kneeling before Him. This respectful approach showed acknowledgement for God as the ultimate king authority. When the people saw the positive attitude of their king, they were encouraged to do the same. In another example, when Abraham's servant knew God had answered his prayer, he bowed down and worshipped the Lord, saying, *"Praise is to the Lord, the God of my master Abraham, who has not abandoned His kindness and faithfulness to my servant. As for me, the Lord has led me to my master's relative"* (Genesis 24:27).

POSTRATING IN PRAYER

Prostrating in prayer is an attitude commonly practiced in many cultures as a sign of respect and submission. It involves throwing oneself flat on the ground in surrender. This posture is also adopted in prayer as a way to express total surrender to Almighty God, saying, "Lord, I give up everything in surrender to Your way and Your will." Another example of kneeling in supplication can be found in Joshua 5:4.

Prostrating or falling on the knees, bowing forward, resting on the hands or elbows, with the head touching the ground, is a way to show reverence in prayer. The worshipper may also lift their face upwards, as mentioned in Job 22:26: *"Surely then you will find delight in the Almighty and will lift up your face to God."*

In the early Christian community, there were instances where people mistakenly offered homage to the apostles prostrating before them, such as in the case of Peter and Cornelius. When Cornelius fell at Peter's feet in reverence, Peter immediately redirected him to Christ, refusing to accept the glory and acknowledging that he was only a man. The apostles understood that any power or miracles they performed were not their own, but were the work of God. They consistently directed people's worship and gratitude towards Jehovah God through Jesus Christ (Acts 10:26).

SITTING IN PRAYER

Sitting is another posture employed in prayer. The petitioner may kneel and then sit back upon their knee in prayer. From this position, they could bow their head or rest it on their bosom. In times of extreme distress, falling on one's face is often a way to express deep sorrow. Additionally, wearing sackcloth or a shawl while approaching God with reverence and godly fear is another way to show respect. It is crucial to remember that God is far above all other gods and to approach Him with a humble heart. Prostrating or falling on the knees, bowing forward, resting on hands or elbows, with the head touching the ground, is a way to demonstrate reverence.

EMBRACING PRAYER IN VARIOUS FORMS AND PRACTICES

The most important attitude we can have in prayer is one of a right heart. Its position supercedes that of any physical position. Jesus prayed and looked towards heaven, demonstrating a steadfast heart towards His Father. He also prayed publicly but emphasised that it is important to do so in sincerity. He cautioned against making long prayers for show, as some scribes did. Instead, he emphasised the importance of genuine and humble prayer (Luke 20:47).

In Ezekiel's prayerful vision, he witnessed twenty-five men bowing in prayer with their backs towards the temple of God, their faces turned towards the East (Ezekiel 8:16). This act carried significant symbolism as temples of sun worshippers were constructed with entrances on the left side, where worshippers would face the rising sun. However, the worshippers of God deliberately turned their backs on the rising sun, acknowledging that true worship should be directed towards the living God, not created celestial bodies.

The Apostle Paul encouraged people to be thankful in all circumstances, recognising that evil does not come from God. Even in the face of adversity, expressing gratitude for God's presence and goodness is important. God can bring about good through distress. Paul also urged persistence in prayer, even during times when it may seem lengthy, as it is an expression of faith in God's faithfulness to answer prayers.

It is worth noting that prayers can be made silently, without outward expressions. Nevertheless, in every form of supplication to the Lord, prayer should be embraced alongside other aspects of the Christian armour and accompanied by all graces. Prayer should become an integral part of our lives—praying always, maintaining a constant and fervent spirit of prayer, persevering in prayer, and keeping our hearts in a prayerful state. The physical position during prayer may vary, with examples ranging from kneeling to even lying face down on the ground, as Hezekiah did in his deep grief when he turned his face to the wall. Again, let us remember to do so in sincerity.

We should go about our day with a prayerful heart. This makes us ready to engage in spontaneous short prayers throughout the day. There are moments when immediate prayers are needed before a specific task or in times of emergency. During such occasions, it is essential to cultivate the practice of brief prayers, keeping them concise yet heartfelt. By planning our lives around God's teachings on prayer and homage, our very existence can become a continuous offering of prayer—a lifestyle encompassing prayer in all its forms (Ephesians 6:18).

May our prayers be characterised by a humble heart, unwavering faith, and a deep desire to align our lives with God's will.

Eleven

Attitudes Towards Religious Gestures

Religious gestures have long been an integral part of worshipping God. They serve as powerful expressions of devotion, reverence, and communion with God. From bowed heads and folded hands to kneeling, removing of shoes, and covering our heads, these gestures carry deep symbolic meaning and offer a tangible way to express our hearts to God. But what should our attitudes be towards them? Understanding the answer to this question will help ensure that they are placed in their proper place and aligned with their intended meaning.

CLAPPING HANDS: EXPRESSION, CELEBRATION, AND WORSHIP

The act of clapping hands holds various meanings and purposes. People clap their hands to express joy, lift their voices towards heaven, worship, or even engage in physical exercise for good health. Clapping can create a warm atmosphere of joy and togetherness, especially when done in the right attitude. In some instances, clapping hands is used as a form of creating music in worship, as in many Pentecostal worship services. The Psalmist David invited all nations to clap their hands and shout to God with cries of joy, acknowledging the greatness of the Lord Most High.

SANDAL REMOVAL: RESPECT AND REVERENCE

Removing one's sandals carries symbolic significance as a gesture of respect and reverence. In the encounter between God and Moses at the burning bush, God commanded Moses to remove his sandals because the ground he stood on was holy. It demonstrated Moses' acknowledgement of his own unworthiness before the sovereign Lord. Similarly, in the tabernacle and temple, the priests performed their duties barefooted, considering these places as holy. Removing footwear when entering religious buildings or as a sign of respect in various cultures is still practiced today.

WASHING OF FEET: SIGNS OF HUMILITY AND HONOUR

The act of washing hands or feet is deeply rooted in Eastern customs and holds spiritual meaning. It signifies humility and service towards others. Pouring water on another's hands, as seen in the example of Elijah and Elisha, was a practice performed after a meal and represented hospitality and respect. Washing feet was an act of humility and service, exemplified by Jesus when he washed the feet of his disciples. He demonstrated that true leadership is about humility and serving others, setting an example for believers to follow.

There is a spirit of humility in the act of washing one another's feet, which is predominantly practiced in some churches. However, the religious attitude towards this practice can sometimes result in negative attitudes, with some individuals segregating themselves and only choosing to wash the feet of those they deem to have the cleanest and most worthy feet. Others may limit their service to washing the feet of beggars, the lame, or those they consider beneath them.

In a true story, there was a designated day for washing one another's feet during a church service. On this day, a mother chose to wash her daughter's feet, and in return, the daughter washed her mother's feet while some people looked on in disgust. They did not appreciate the meaning of this gesture, thinking perhaps that the two ought not to have washed each other's feet, but this served as an example, employing one of the ancient customs, to teach a lesson in humility and serving one another. Jesus, too, washed the feet of His disciples. He wrapped a towel around His waist, assuming the role of the lowest slave, and washed and dried His disciples' feet. Peter watched this act and witnessed Jesus behaving like a servant. Until then, Peter had not fully understood Jesus' teachings that one must be willing to be a servant before becoming a leader. This statement and action are uncomfortable for some leaders who may consider serving those they deem below their standards. Jesus left this example for His followers to practice as they carried out their mission among believers.

The positive side of the illustration of washing one another's feet lies in helping and serving fellow believers with humility. Jesus, as an example, washed the feet of His disciples. When Peter asked Jesus not only to wash his feet but also his hands and head, Jesus replied, *"He who is bathed does not need to wash, except for his feet, but is completely clean"* (see John 13:9-10). Peter initially objected to Jesus' demonstration of washing one another's feet, but Jesus helped him understand the significance of humility. Jesus used the example of taking a bath and returning home, only needing to wash the dust from one's sandaled feet. He used this as a figurative representation of spiritual cleansing from the pollution of sin. By washing His disciples' feet, Jesus showed His love and stooped down to wash the feet of His followers, making this act known to the entire world. Rising from supper and to the great surprise of the company, Christ washed His disciples' feet while fully aware of His exalted state and all the honours that came with it.

Judas, the one who betrayed Jesus, was present when Jesus washed His disciples' feet. Jesus was washing the feet of a sinner, the worst of sinners. This act serves as an example, just as Abraham showed zealous hospitality to three guests by providing water in a basin to wash their feet. This was necessary due to the dusty roads they traveled on. It is evident that individuals in dire poverty, who cannot afford proper footwear, have a greater need to wash off the daily dirt from their feet before going to bed, especially after walking on dusty roads in poor weather conditions. In such cases, their feet need to be washed by someone else.

A person's reputation was closely tied to hospitality, including the act of sharing and providing food. Even strangers were to be treated as highly honoured guests when meeting their needs for food and shelter. It is one of the most immediate and practical ways of obeying God. Like Abraham, one should be open to entertaining angels, although this thought should not be constantly on one's mind, but rather as an opportunity to meet the needs of strangers (Genesis 18:4).

HOSPITALITY AND REPUTATION

Hospitality played a significant role in the lives of believers, both in the Old Testament and the early Christian community. It was considered a virtue and an essential aspect of demonstrating love and care for others. In the Bible, there are numerous examples of individuals who extended hospitality and were commended for their actions.

A person's reputation was often closely connected to their practice of hospitality. In ancient times, sharing and providing food for others, especially strangers, was seen as a way to honour and show respect. Even strangers were to be treated as highly honoured guests, and meeting their needs through the provision of food and shelter was regarded as one of the most immediate and practical ways of obeying God's commandments.

Abraham stands as a prime example of someone who exemplified hospitality. In Genesis 18, when three visitors approached his tent, Abraham eagerly welcomed them and showed great hospitality by offering them food and refreshment. He went above and beyond in serving them, even preparing a feast with the help of his wife Sarah. Little did Abraham know that these visitors were actually angels sent by God. His act of hospitality not only demonstrated his generosity but also brought about blessings and divine revelations.

In the New Testament, hospitality continued to hold importance in the early Christian community. Believers were encouraged to show hospitality to one another and to strangers. The Apostle Paul, in his letter to the Romans, exhorted the believers to "practice hospitality" (Romans 12:13). The author of the letter to the Hebrews also emphasised the significance of hospitality by urging the readers to show love to strangers, as some have entertained angels without even knowing it (Hebrews 13:2).

Hospitality was not merely a cultural custom or social obligation but a reflection of the believers' faith and their commitment to following the teachings of Christ. By opening their homes and providing for others, they demonstrated Christ-like love and care. It was a tangible expression of their willingness to serve and meet the needs of others, regardless of their social status or background.

The act of hospitality went beyond providing physical nourishment. It created an environment of warmth, acceptance, and fellowship, fostering relationships and deepening the sense of community among believers. It was an opportunity to share the good news of the gospel and to witness the transformative power of God's love.

In today's world, the call to practice hospitality remains relevant. It extends beyond the confines of church walls and encompasses various forms of kindness and generosity shown to others. It may involve inviting someone into our homes, sharing a meal, providing assistance to those in need, or simply offering a listening ear and a compassionate heart.

By practicing hospitality, believers have the opportunity to reflect the love of Christ and make a positive impact on the lives of others. It not only enriches relationships but also contributes to the building of a community rooted in love, compassion, and mutual support. May we continue to embrace the spirit of hospitality, following the example set by Christ and the early believers, as we seek to extend care and welcome to all those we encounter on our journey of faith.

LAYING ON OF HANDS

Laying on of hands is an ancient Jewish practice that involves setting individuals apart for special services or designating them for specific offices or duties. This can be seen in the appointment of the seven men chosen by the apostles to oversee food distribution in the congregation at Jerusalem. Timothy, known for his right attitude, was appointed to oversee older men in the congregation. He, in turn, was entrusted by an elder to make appointments for overseeing others, emphasising the importance of considering positive attitudes in choosing church leaders (Titus 1:5-9).

In the early church, men were ordained or commissioned and set apart through prayer and the laying on of hands by the apostles. This practice signified the work of the Holy Spirit in making these delicate choices. The Apostle Paul taught that the laying on of hands was a way to designate certain benefits or power to flow as the Spirit came upon those whom hands were laid upon. It is important to note that this does not mean the Spirit passed through the hands of Paul. Rather, as a representative of Christ, Paul was authorised to designate, in accordance with the requirements for receiving the gifts of the Spirit. However, in the New Testament, the laying on of hands was not always necessary to transmit the gifts of the Spirit. For example, when Cornelius and his household were saved after hearing the gospel, they received the baptism of the Holy Spirit at the moment of their belief without the laying on of hands (Acts 10:44-48). Luke, the writer, tells us that the Holy Spirit fell on all who heard the message while Peter was speaking. The Jewish believers who had accompanied Peter were astonished that the gift of the Holy Spirit had been poured out even on the Gentiles. Peter then commanded that they should be baptised in water in the name of Jesus Christ.

The laying on of hands was a common practice in the Old Testament, even in the selection of animals for sacrifice. The chosen animal had to be clean and consecrated, and the priest would lay his hand on its head in preparation for use. Another example is when Israel reached out his right hand and placed it on Ephraim's head, even though Ephraim was the younger. Jacob crossed his hands and put his left hand on Manasseh's head, despite Manasseh being the firstborn. This act demonstrated an attitude of trust in God's providence and care, as seen in Jacob's example (Genesis 48:14).

Jesus also practiced the laying on of hands when little children were brought to Him to receive His blessings and prayers (Mark 10:16). The disciples, displaying a wrong attitude, rebuked those who brought the children to Jesus. However, Jesus loved the children because they possessed the kind of attitude necessary to approach God. Their childlike trust in God and their receptive hearts served as a great example to the religious leaders who allowed education and sophistication to hinder simple faith in God.

HEAD COVERING

Another religious gesture mentioned in 1 Corinthians 11:5-6 is head covering. In the Old Testament, the custom of head covering was strongly practiced among worshippers, and this same custom was followed in the Christian congregation in the New Testament era. There was a need for explanations and discussions on the subject of Christian head covering among the new believers. Christian women in the congregation were expected to wear head coverings during worship services, as it was a sign of respect in their attire when praying.

The Apostle Paul stated, "But I want you to realize that the head of every man is Christ, and the head of the woman is man, and the head of Christ is God. Every man who prays or prophesies with his head covered dishonours his head. But every woman who prays or prophesies with her head uncovered dishonours her head—it is the same as having her head shaved." (1 Corinthians 11:3-5)

When it comes to women praying and wearing head coverings, Paul outlined an important principle to consider in our attitude towards worship. He taught that if a woman prays without covering her head, it is like she is cutting off her hair. But if it is seen as inappropriate for a woman to cut off her hair, then she should cover her head. The reason behind this is that the man is considered the head of the woman. The mention of women's hair being shaved is used as a metaphor to highlight the importance of head coverings as a symbol of submission and modesty in the context of worship. This discussion about head coverings doesn't imply control or superiority, but rather acknowledges the order of creation. Man was created first, and woman was formed from man. In the same way, man's source is Christ, and Christ's source is God.

God simply enforced submission among equals; He did not make man superior. He made a way for both man and his wife to work together as one, equally under God. The wife should submit to her husband for the sake of marriage and family. Christ was equal with His Father, and His submission led Him to carry out the plan for salvation.

When the Apostle Paul was addressing immoderations in worship and liberating the Corinthians' conversations about head coverings and hair length, he modified certain practices. Paul advised believers to behave in honourable ways in their culture and encouraged them not to adopt practices from other cultures that could distract from their ultimate goal of being witnesses for Jesus Christ. While the custom of men wearing long hair was considered appropriate and masculine in some cultures, in the Corinthian church, it was seen as a cultural sign of male prostitutes in pagan temples. Similarly, women wearing short hair were categorised as prostitutes.

Paul instructed Christian women to keep their hair long if they already had long hair. Some women may prefer to shorten their hair to appear more masculine or for convenience in managing it. This instruction was not meant to teach

Christians to reject godly practices from different cultures but to avoid appearances and behaviours that could distract from their ultimate goal of being witnesses for Jesus Christ (see 1 Corinthians 11:3-9).

The practice of head covering in worship, as taught by Paul, served as a sign of respect, submission, and the proper order of authority within the family and the church community.

As a reminder, religious gestures such as hospitality, the laying on of hands, and head covering carry deep significance in various faith traditions. These practices not only serve as outward expressions of devotion and reverence but also hold profound spiritual meanings. Hospitality reflects the importance of selfless service and care for others, while the laying on of hands symbolises the setting apart of individuals for special roles or the bestowal of spiritual blessings. Head covering, in its cultural and religious context, represents respect and submission. These gestures remind elievers of their commitments, reinforce their faith, and foster a deeper connection with God. As we explore and appreciate these practices, we gain insights into the rich tapestry of religious traditions and the profound ways in which they shape the lives of their adherents.

In addition to the religious gestures of hospitality, the laying on of hands, and head covering, this chapter has also touched upon other significant practices that hold deep meaning within various faith traditions. Hand clapping, for instance, serves as a form of joyful expression, exalting and praising the divine. It symbolises unity, celebration, and reverence in worship settings. The act of removing sandals signifies reverence and humility in the presence of the sacred. It is a way of acknowledging the holy ground upon which one stands and embracing a posture of respect and submission. Lastly, the washing of feet exemplifies the spirit of humility and service, as seen in the teachings and actions of Jesus Christ. It is a powerful symbol of selflessness and a call to compassionately care for others. These additional practices further enrich our understanding of the diverse ways in which religious individuals engage with their faith and connect with the Lord God Almighty.

Twelve

Attitudes Between Siblings

I n the story of Cain and Abel, we witness the power of attitudes and how they can impact relationships, even between close family members. Their story can be found in the Bible in the book of Genesis, specifically Genesis 4:1-16. Both young men were instructed to bring offerings to God, but their attitudes and actions differed greatly.

Abel, a shepherd, approached God with a humble and sincere heart. He carefully selected the finest and healthiest of his flock as his offering, demonstrating his reverence and respect for God. Abel's attitude reflected his understanding of God's worthiness and his desire to give his best.

On the other hand, Cain, a farmer, had a different attitude. He brought an offering of his produce to God, but it lacked the same level of sincerity and thoughtfulness as Abel's offering. Cain did not give his best or choose his offering with reverence. His attitude was marked by complacency and a lack of true devotion.

As a result, God accepted Abel's offering but did not regard Cain or his offering with favour. This rejection stirred negative emotions within Cain. Instead of examining his own attitude and seeking to improve, he became angry and resentful towards his brother. He allowed envy and jealousy to take root in his heart, fueling his discontentment.

God, in His mercy, confronted Cain about his attitude and warned him of the consequences of harboring such negative emotions. God encouraged Cain to choose the right path, advising him that if he did what was right, he would be accepted. God's plea to Cain was an opportunity for him to repent, change his attitude, and offer a sincere and pleasing sacrifice.

However, Cain refused to heed God's counsel. His heart hardened, and he allowed his negative attitude to prevail. In his hardened state, he plotted and carried out a heinous act - he murdered his own brother Abel. This act of violence was a tragic outcome of Cain's unchecked anger, envy, and unwillingness to address his attitude.

The story of Cain and Abel serves as a sobering reminder of the significance of attitudes and their potential consequences. It teaches us the importance of approaching God with sincerity, reverence, and a desire to give our best. It also warns us about the dangers of allowing negative attitudes like envy, jealousy, and anger to take root in our hearts. Ultimately, the story reminds us of the need to choose the path of righteousness and to address our attitudes before they lead us down destructive paths.

JACOB AND ESAU: TRICKED OUT OF A BIRTHRIGHT

There is another well-known story in the Bible that illustrates the destructive power of jealousy, particularly within the context of brotherhood. The story I am referring to can be found in the book of Genesis, specifically in Genesis 25:19-34. It recounts the account of Esau and Jacob, two brothers whose relationship was strained by jealousy and a conflict over the birthright. A birthright is a special honour given to the first-born son, in this case, Esau, which included a double portion of the family inheritance and the role of leader in the family. Esau had the option to sell or give away his birthright, but doing so would mean losing both material goods and his leadership position.

Unbeknown to Esau, Jacob, driven by his ambition and aided by their mother, Rebekah, deceived their father, Isaac, and took the birthright blessings meant for Esau. But, unfortunately, Esau made this easier because he disregarded the spiritual blessings that would have come with his birthright and despised it. One day, he came from the countryside and saw his younger brother Jacob cooking. "Quick, let me have some of the red stew! I'm famished!" Esau said. In response, his brother said, "Sell me your birthright." Immediately, without considering its value and the consequences of parting with the birthright, Esau replied, "Look, I am about to die. What good is the birthright to me?" So Esau swore an oath to sell his birthright to Jacob. He traded the lasting benefits of his birthright for the immediate but shorterm pleasure of food. The greedy brother's hasty attitude focused on satisfying his immediate desires without considering the long-term consequences.

Once Esau realised the consequences of his actions, he became filled with anger, bitterness, and jealousy towards Jacob and plotted to kill his brother. The rivalry and animosity between the brothers continued as they both sought their father's blessing, and Jacob had to flee to escape Esau's wrath.

The story illustrates how jealousy can lead to deep divisions and strained relationships, even among family members. Esau's jealousy towards Jacob stemmed from a sense of betrayal and a perceived loss of what was rightfully his. His intense emotions and desire for revenge highlight the destructive power of jealousy.

Furthermore, the consequences of their jealousy and conflict extended beyond their personal relationship. It affected their entire family and had long-lasting effects on their descendants, shaping the future conflicts between the nations descended from them. Overall, the story of Esau and Jacob can be seen as a cautionary tale about the destructive nature of jealousy and the harmful consequences it can have on relationships and families.

Esau's focus on his hunger made it easier for him to disregard the inheritance. Similar feelings of pressure can arise in situations like sexual temptation, where a married vow may seem unimportant. Overcoming temptation in such pressure-filled moments can be the most difficult.

THE PRODIGAL SON: A TALE OF JEALOUSY AND REDEMPTION

The story of the prodigal son, found in Luke 15:11-32, depicts the relationship between two brothers and showcases the themes of jealousy and resentment. The parable begins with a younger son who asks his father for his share of the inheritance and goes on to squander it in wild living. When the younger son reaches rock bottom and realises his mistakes, he decides to return to his father, hoping to be treated as a hired servant. However, upon seeing his son's return, the father eagerly welcomes him back with open arms, throwing a grand celebration.

The older brother, who remained faithful to his father and worked diligently, becomes jealous and resentful when he hears about the lavish reception given to his younger brother. He feels that his efforts and loyalty have been overlooked and overshadowed. In his anger, the older brother refuses to join the celebration and confronts his father. He expresses his bitterness and questions why he has never received such treatment despite his faithfulness.

This story highlights the destructive nature of jealousy and resentment within the context of sibling relationships. The older brother's envy blinds him to the joy of his brother's return and the father's love. It reveals the deep-seated resentment that can arise when one feels overlooked or unappreciated. The parable challenges the listener to reflect on their own attitudes and reminds them of the importance of forgiveness, compassion, and the need to overcome jealousy and resentment.

Ultimately, the story serves as a reminder of God's boundless love and mercy, as depicted by the forgiving and compassionate father in the parable. It encourages us to let go of resentment, embrace reconciliation, and extend grace towards others, even when they have seemingly fallen short or caused us pain.

These examples serve as reminders of the dangers of harbouring jealousy and resentment in our hearts. They caution us against allowing these negative emotions to fester and consume us, for they can lead to harm, both physically and emotionally. Instead, we are called to cultivate a spirit of love, forgiveness, and reconciliation, seeking harmony and unity in our relationships. By recognising and addressing our wrong attitudes, we can pave the way for healing, growth, and restoration.

JOSEPH: HOW A DREAM CAME BETWEEN BROTHERS

Joseph, among his many brothers, unfortunately became the target of their jealous attitudes. In a family, brothers are meant to support and care for one another, especially when a younger sibling is born. Joseph's positive attitude was marked by natural confidence, self-assurance, and determination. However, as Joseph became the favoured son of their father, his know-it-all attitude towards his brothers grew increasingly unbearable. This only fueled their jealousy, and they conspired against him.

There was a significant contrast between Joseph and his brothers. Joseph had a personal relationship with God, which allowed him to thrive and prosper where his brothers would have faltered. He was blessed with wisdom, confidence, and the ability to win the hearts of those around him. Unfortunately, the situation took a turn for the worse when their father made Joseph a robe of many colours, a clear symbol of favouritism that further strained the relationship with his brothers. Favouritism within a family should be avoided, as it often leads to jealousy and potentially harmful consequences. Already angered and fueled by Joseph's immaturity and boastful behaviour, his brothers plotted to kill him, ultimately deciding to sell him into slavery instead.

After enduring several years of hardship, Joseph learned a crucial lesson: his talents and knowledge were gifts from God. Over time, he emerged as a leader among his captors. The deep-seated jealousy of his brothers transformed into raging anger, blinding them to what was right. However, in the end, Joseph overcame every pitfall, temptation, and obstacle. He was elevated to a position of leadership, becoming the overseer of his once-jealous brothers.

The story of Joseph and his brothers serves as a poignant reminder of the destructive power of jealousy and the importance of cultivating positive attitudes. It highlights the consequences of favouritism within families and the need for humility, forgiveness, and reconciliation. Joseph's journey teaches us the value of trusting in God's plan, even in the face of adversity. By recognising and addressing our own jealous tendencies, we can strive for healthy relationships, growth, and ultimately, restoration.

The spirit of jealousy is defined as exacting, exclusive, intolerant, rivalrous, unfaithful, envious, suspicious, and apparent. An individual with a jealous attitude can be a destructive force ruling the heart. If jealousy finds its way into the heart, it brings along other destructive forces, causing indifference towards others and leading to sinful habits. This kind of attitude can have both positive and negative consequences, powerful enough to cause death, envy, and upset in friendships and families. It can be difficult to discern the attitude of a person who is jealous because actions speak louder than words.

Jealous behaviour can manifest in different ways among individuals. People may develop jealous attitudes for various reasons, such as longing to possess qualities they perceive in others, desiring different circumstances, or harbouring resentment and discontentment. However, God, in His wisdom, warns against the sin of idolatry and calls us to avoid making idols and practicing devotion towards them. God's name represents righteousness, holiness, purity, uprightness, and unwavering loyalty in the highest degree and must be regarded exclusively.

In the context of jealousy, idolatry can occur when we place our desires, aspirations, or the pursuit of worldly possessions above our devotion to God. Instead of embracing our unique identities and being content with who we are, we may become consumed by comparison and envy. This not only leads us away from God's intended path for us but also hinders our ability to appreciate and celebrate the blessings in our own lives.

God's commandments serve as a guide for us to cultivate virtuous attitudes and resist the temptations of jealousy. By focusing on developing qualities such as gratitude, contentment, and humility, we can overcome jealous tendencies and align ourselves with God's character. It is through seeking a relationship with Him and aligning our hearts with His attributes that we can find true fulfillment and discover our unique purpose.

RACHEL AND LEAH: JEALOUSY AMONG SISTERS

In Genesis 29:31-30:24, we encounter the story of Rachel, one of Jacob's wives, who was deeply affected by her barrenness and her yearning to compete with her sister for Jacob's affection. The rivalry between the two sisters was marked by a relentless desire to bear more children than the other. In their desperation, the sisters even resorted to giving their maidservants to Jacob as concubines in the hope of increasing their offspring. However, Jacob, recognising his deep love for Rachel, wisely refused. Yet, Rachel's attempts to win her husband's love through the birth of a child reflect a more profound error.

Rachel's inability to conceive ignited a fiery jealousy within her, poisoning her attitude towards her sister Leah. This serves as a poignant example of the destructive nature of jealousy, breeding bitterness, envy, and an unhealthy sense of competition. Rachel's jealous disposition cast a dark shadow over her relationship with Leah, deteriorating her connection with her husband as well. Frustrated and disheartened, Rachel expressed her desperation to Jacob, uttering the poignant words, "Give me children, or I'll die."

In her anguish, Rachel failed to grasp that her husband's devotion was not contingent upon her ability to bear children. She was consumed by her pain and disappointment, eagerly anticipating signs of pregnancy each month only to be met with further despair. She may have harbored resentment towards her husband for his attentiveness to Leah, who was able to conceive. Rachel silently endured her suffering, yet she made her anguish known, seeking solace and assistance.

Rachel had yet to come to terms with the understanding that children are a precious gift from the Lord, and she needed to patiently await her appointed time. In the midst of her longing, she had to confront and transform her attitude towards her sister, her husband, and God. When Jacob heard of Rachel's deep desire for children, he responded with humility, saying, "Am I in the place of God, who has kept you from having children?" Ultimately, in God's providence, Rachel's prayer was answered, and she gave birth to a child of her own.

The story of Rachel reminds us of the dangers of jealousy and the destructive impact it can have on relationships. It also serves as a call to shift our focus from seeking validation and love from others to finding fulfillment and unconditional love in our relationship with Jesus Christ. When we turn to Him, we can experience the boundless love and acceptance that surpasses any earthly measure, bringing healing and restoration to our hearts and relationships.

JEALOUSY AMONG SPIRITUAL BROTHERS AND SISTERS

A jealous attitude can be devastating, whether among parents, children, mothers, fathers, leaders, followers, employers, and employees. When an individual suddenly expresses fits of jealousy, their behaviour can lead to unnecessary blame, anger, fights, and other harmful actions. It is important to avoid and shun such destructive behaviour by heeding the Word of God, which can keep your mind in perfect peace. Do not give in to temptation or lose control.

The Apostle Paul spoke of fellow believers as his spiritual brothers, likening them to a virgin engaged to Christ as His prospective bride. In the Bible, Christ is depicted as a jealous husband over His Church of believers as a way to convey the depth of God's love, commitment, and desire for a faithful relationship with His people. This metaphor portrays God's longing for undivided devotion and loyalty from His followers. Just as a husband expects faithfulness and exclusivity from his wife, God desires His people to worship Him alone and not turn to other gods or idols. This metaphor emphasises the importance of a genuine, wholehearted relationship with God, and warns against spiritual unfaithfulness and idolatry. It reveals God's protective and possessive nature towards His people, ensuring that they remain steadfast in their devotion to Him.

In his letters, Paul consistently addressed the attitudes of the early church, especially emphasising their relationships as brethren (for example, see 1 Corinthians 1:10; Ephesians 4:1-3; Philippians 2:2-4). With great zeal and genuine concern, Paul passionately urged the Corinthians to transform their negative attitudes into positive ones. He recognised the vital importance of fostering a spirit of unity, love, and mutual respect among the believers. Paul understood that the attitudes within the church community significantly impacted their interactions and the overall effectiveness of their witness to the world. Through his heartfelt letters, he encouraged them to embrace humility, forgiveness, and genuine care for one another, promoting a harmonious and Christ-centred fellowship among the brethren. Paul's exhortations serve as a timeless reminder for all believers to prioritise nurturing healthy attitudes and fostering genuine brotherly love within the church. The Christian life requires hard work, patience, understanding, and not giving up hastily, endangering one's relationship with God. We must choose to patiently struggle against sin, with the power of the Holy Spirit, and rise above jealousy. Negative attitudes can drive others away without the person even saying a word, as is often the case among believers today.

For instance, allowing bickering to dominate your love for one another while the devil stirs up disagreements, differing opinions, arguments, and rivalries. These negative attitudes harm goodwill, trust, and peace, hindering progress towards important goals. Such attitudes may prevent other believers from wholeheartedly cooperating in the congregation due to self-centredness. Jesus understood the distracted behaviour that exists among believers, and in His final prayer, He prayed to His Father that believers may become one in Him (see John 17:2).

LISTEN TO THE WARNING LIGHT

Like a warning light shining brightly, bad attitudes can lead to a dead end. Stop, count to ten, take a deep breath, and allow your conscience to speak louder than a voice, guiding you on what to do next. Since you know how dangerous the spirit of jealousy can become, guard yourself against selfishness, prejudice, or jealousy that may lead to dissension. Show genuine positivity towards others instead. Many people of all races and genders are behind prison bars because they ignored their inner voice and accepted wrong advice.

The positive attitude of active listening has great benefits and leads to positive outcomes. Individuals who practice listening and follow the right instructions are wise. It is always a downfall for those who refuse to listen. Many parents mourn the wrong choices made by their children, realising that being stricter with them in the first place and guiding them towards positive choices would have yielded better outcomes.

There is a right and wrong way to navigate through life's journey. Stop for a moment to read the signposts for directions. A jealous attitude can be disastrous for various reasons. It doesn't make sense, as this attitude has the ability to lead people into confusion and delusion. When Saul was driven to insanity and sought to murder David, David played music to minister to King Saul and bring relief from his evil spirit. However, driven by his jealousy towards David, King Saul threw his spear at him, narrowly missing David as he played. If left unchecked, a jealous attitude can quickly grow and lead to murder. His jealousy blinded him to the fact that David was an important and faithful ally. It is important to deal with jealousy at the right time by first examining your own attitude so that you can better address others.

Thirteen

Attitudes Between
Man and His Wife

Marital jealousy is a natural response when a husband feels uneasy or concerned upon seeing his wife engage in pleasant interactions with other men. It is reasonable for a husband to expect his wife to prioritise their relationship and show exclusive devotion to him. This form of jealousy can be seen as a protective attitude, where a husband cherishes his wife and guards her as a precious treasure. In a similar way, God, as a jealous husband, passionately protects His chosen people and regards any harm to them as a personal affront.

God's jealousy is not rooted in insecurity or possessiveness but stems from His pure love for His creation. His jealousy is driven by His zealous commitment to establish righteousness and protect His name. Within the Christian congregation, it is essential to cultivate a godly form of jealousy towards fellow believers. This involves desiring to assist them, earnestly praying for their well-being, and maintaining an unwavering devotion to God.

Jealousy is a powerful emotion that can deeply impact both the mind and the heart. It possesses the potential to be more destructive than anger or rage, as it can linger, take root, and be difficult to appease. However, while a righteous individual might respond with anger when faced with certain situations, God's jealousy remains pure and untainted, motivated by His boundless love for His people.

STANDING WHEN YOU LACK SUPPORT

In a story set in heaven, Satan accused a man named Job before the court, and the judge acknowledged the injustice (see the book of Job). Satan, driven by his cruel agenda, mercilessly challenged Job's integrity, aiming to break his faith. Even in the face of immense suffering and loss, Job's wife, influenced by despair, urged him to renounce his faith and curse God. However, Job demonstrated remarkable strength and unwavering conviction as he clung to his integrity, remaining faithful to God. Job's unwavering faith and steadfastness in the midst of adversity serve as a powerful example of the positive attitude that can strengthen the bond between husband and wife, even when one partner may struggle with despair and doubts. In the Bible, we see examples of different attitudes between husbands and wives that can serve as lessons for us today. One such example is found in the story of Abraham and Sarah. In Genesis 16, Sarah, who was unable to bear children, became impatient and suggested that Abraham have a child with her maidservant, Hagar. This decision stemmed from Sarah's desire to fulfill God's promise of descendants for Abraham. However, instead of waiting for God's timing, Sarah's attitude of impatience led to conflict and complications within their household. It highlights the importance of trusting in God's promises and having patience and unity in marriage, even in the face of challenges.

Another example can be seen in the relationship between Aquila and Priscilla, a married couple mentioned in the New Testament. In Acts 18, they are described as faithful believers who worked together as tentmakers and served as mentors to Apollos, helping him understand the way of God more accurately. Their attitude towards each other and their shared dedication to God's work demonstrate a beautiful partnership and mutual support in their marriage. They exemplify the importance of unity, teamwork, and using their strengths and gifts to build up the Kingdom of God together.

These examples remind us that attitudes between husbands and wives can significantly impact the dynamics of a marriage. It emphasises the need for patience, trust, unity, mutual support, and a shared commitment to God's purposes. By learning from these biblical examples, we can cultivate positive attitudes in our own marriages, fostering love, understanding, and a strong foundation for a fulfilling relationship.

Attitudes between husband and wife are crucial in every stage of marriage, including the challenges faced by ageing couples. As time goes by and physical limitations may increase, it becomes even more important to cultivate positive attitudes rooted in faith and love. Just as Job remained steadfast in his integrity despite suffering (Job 2:9) and Habakkuk rejoiced in the Lord despite adverse circumstances (Habakkuk 3:17), couples of any age can choose to embrace a positive attitude, relying on God's strength and purpose.

Negative attitudes within a marriage can deeply impact the emotional well-being of both spouses. When one partner harbors negative attitudes such as resentment, frustration, or neglect, it can inadvertently make the other feel unloved or undervalued. However, it is crucial for couples to remember that God's love for them is unwavering and unending. He has loved them with an everlasting love (Jeremiah 31:3) and demonstrated His ultimate love by sacrificing His Son for their redemption (John 3:16).

EMBRACE GOD'S LOVE

By embracing God's love and extending it to one another, couples can overcome the challenges that negative attitudes may present. It is essential to actively nurture an atmosphere of love, respect, and gratitude within the marriage. Through open communication, understanding, and forgiveness, couples can foster an environment where negative attitudes are replaced by appreciation and affection. They can find solace and strength in God's unfailing support, knowing that His grace is sufficient for every situation (2 Corinthians 12:9).

Regardless of age, couples can choose to replace negative attitudes with expressions of love and kindness. By intentionally demonstrating care, affirmation, and encouragement, they can cultivate a deep sense of love and belonging within the marriage. Such positive attitudes not only uplift and nourish the emotional well-being of each spouse but also serve as a powerful testimony to the enduring love and faithfulness of God.

As couples of any age embrace a positive attitude towards one another, they create a space where love flourishes, emotional needs are met, and their relationship thrives. In the journey of marriage, anchored in God's love, couples can experience the joy, contentment, and strength that come from a mutual commitment to love, cherish, and support one another. By daily choosing a positive attitude grounded in faith, couples can create a lasting legacy of love that reflects the transformative power of God's love within their marriage.

GOD'S POWER IS SUFFICIENT

Though God may not always remove physical afflictions or limitations, as in the case of the Apostle Paul, He promises to demonstrate His mighty power in our weaknesses (2 Corinthians 12:9). Recognising our limitations can actually lead to a deeper reliance on God and allow Him to develop our Christian character in His strength.

When you feel incapable of fulfilling expectations or have experienced failures, remember that you can do all things through Christ who strengthens you (Philippians 4:13). Just as Jesus directed the disciples to cast their nets on the right side, seek the guidance of the Holy Spirit in finding the right path and allowing Him to lead you to God's purposes (John 21:6).

In times when you may grow weary in doing good without immediate results or acknowledgement, do not give up. Trust in God's timing and His promise that you will reap a harvest if you do not faint (Galatians 6:9). If you struggle with forgiving yourself or your spouse, remember the kindness and forgiveness that

God has extended to you through Christ, and let it guide your attitude towards others (Ephesians 4:32).

If you find yourself burdened and overwhelmed, cast your burdens upon the Lord, knowing that He will sustain you and keep you steadfast (Psalm 55:22). When fear creeps in, remember that God has not given you a spirit of fear but of power, love, and a sound mind (2 Timothy 1:7).

During times when your faith feels weak, remind yourself that God has given each person a measure of faith and that it is through His grace and provision that you can think soberly and trust in Him (Romans 12:3).

Rather than embracing negative attitudes and unbelief, focus on seeking wisdom and understanding from God. He promises to be with you always, never leaving nor forsaking you (Hebrews 13:5). Let the encouragement and guidance found in God's Word transform your negative attitudes into positive and faith-filled perspectives.

In all aspects of life, including the attitudes we adopt within marriage, we are called to think soberly and humbly, recognising that our faith and abilities come from God's grace. By trusting in His strength and seeking His wisdom, we can navigate the challenges and joys of marriage with a positive attitude, rooted in faith and guided by His Word.

Fourteen

Attitudes of the Pharisees Towards Jesus

I n the days of Jesus' time on earth, there were two prominent sects of religious leaders: the Pharisees and the Sadducees. The Pharisees were a influential and well-known group of religious leaders. They emphasised strict adherence to religious laws and traditions, placing importance on ritual purity and the interpretation of Scripture. The Pharisees took great pride in their religious practices and traditions. They cherished the observance of fasting twice a week, paying tithes, and showcasing their self-righteous attitude by enlarging the fringes on their garments. They had a love for money, desired recognition and titles, and often showed favouritism in their interpretation and application of the Law, burdening the common people. Like the Sadducees, this sect was known for their extensive knowledge of the Jewish law but, unlike the latter, they also kept the oral traditions, which meant that they often found themselves in conflict, differences of opinion and competition with the Sadducees.

The Sadducees were a priestly class that focused primarily on the literal interpretation of the Torah (the first five books of the Old Testament), and rejected the authority of other Jewish texts. They held significant influence within the Temple establishment and were more accommodating to influences of the Roman leaders, which allowed them to maintain their political and religious influence.

During Jesus' ministry, the attitudes of the Pharisees towards Him revealed a stark contrast between their self-centred motives and His selfless mission. As religious leaders, they were supposed to guide people towards God and uphold the principles of righteousness. However, they became preoccupied with their own status and personal gain, which led them to lose sight of their true purpose. Their self-righteousness led them to look down upon others, particularly those who did not adhere to their strict standards. They also clashed with the Sadducees over various beliefs, such as the resurrection, angels, and spirits.

One of the main points of contention between the Pharisees and Jesus was their interpretation and strict adherence to religious traditions, particularly regarding the observance of the Sabbath. Jesus, on the other hand, emphasised the importance of compassion, healing, and meeting people's needs, even on the Sabbath. This clashed with the Pharisees' rigid adherence to the letter of the Law, causing them to resent Jesus and accuse Him of violating their traditions.

Jealousy played a significant role in the Pharisees' negative attitudes towards Jesus. They were envious of His popularity, the miracles He performed, the authority with which He taught, and His association with tax collectors and sinners. Their jealousy blinded them to the truth and hindered them from recognising Jesus as the Messiah.

Jesus and the Sadducees often found themselves in conflict due to their differing beliefs and practices. One of the major points of contention was their disagreement about the concept of life after death. While the Sadducees denied the idea of resurrection and an afterlife, Jesus firmly believed in the resurrection of the dead and the existence of eternal life. This disparity became evident when the Sadducees posed a perplexing question to Jesus, inquiring about a woman who had been married to multiple brothers. Jesus skillfully responded by explaining that in the afterlife, people are like angels and do not marry, illustrating his belief in the resurrection (Matthew 22:23-33, Mark 12:18-27, Luke 20:27-40).

Another significant source of conflict between Jesus and the Sadducees revolved around the temple in Jerusalem. The Sadducees held authoritative positions within the temple and exploited it for their personal gain. However, Jesus passionately opposed such practices. He expressed his displeasure upon witnessing merchants and money changers conducting business within the temple premises and forcefully drove them out, proclaiming the sacred nature of the temple (Matthew 21:12-13, Mark 11:15-18, Luke 19:45-46, John 2:13-16). This action challenged the authority of the Sadducees and exposed their corrupt practices, provoking their anger and animosity towards Jesus.

Additionally, Jesus and the Sadducees clashed over their interpretations and applications of Jewish Law. The Sadducees adhered strictly to the letter of the law, emphasising rituals and rules, while Jesus emphasised the underlying principles of justice, compassion, and faithfulness. Jesus criticised the Sadducees for their excessive focus on legalistic observances, urging them to prioritise matters of justice, mercy, and faithfulness (Matthew 23:23). This fundamental difference in their approaches to the Jewish Law contributed to further discord and disagreement between Jesus and the Sadducees.

Another important group of this time was the Scribes. The Scribes played a key role within the religious and legal framework of Jewish society and were highly educated experts in the interpretation and teaching of Jewish law, or Torah. They held positions of authority and were responsible for studying, preserving, and transmitting the sacred Scriptures, including the laws, teachings, and traditions of Judaism. They served as teachers, legal advisors, and scholars, providing interpretations and rulings on matters of religious and legal importance.

In some instances, the Scribes aligned themselves with the Pharisees and shared their emphasis on religious observance and adherence to the Law. They often collaborated with the Pharisees in maintaining and promoting their understanding of Jewish tradition and practice. However, not all Scribes were aligned with the Pharisees, as there was often diversity of opinions and affiliations even among the Scribes themselves.

The Scribes, who were experts in Jewish law and held influential positions, frequently clashed with Jesus due to his teachings and actions that challenged their authority and interpretation of the law. Jesus criticised the Scribes for their hypocritical practices, highlighting their tendency to prioritise external rituals and appearances over genuine piety and inner transformation. He denounced their excessive emphasis on legalistic observances while neglecting matters of justice, mercy, and faithfulness. Jesus exposed their double standards and called them out for their love of praise and recognition from others rather than seeking the approval of God. The Scribes, feeling threatened by Jesus' popularity and his message of a kingdom that transcended their legalistic framework, became hostile towards him and actively sought to undermine his authority. Their conflict with Jesus exemplifies the clash between his teachings of love, humility, and spiritual truth, and the rigid, self-serving legalism of the Scribes. (See Matthew 23:1-36; Mark 11:27-33; John 8:1-11.)

None of these groups addressed the real problems and needs of the people. The Pharisees emphasised strict adherence to religious laws and traditions, but often neglected matters of the heart and genuine spiritual transformation. The Sadducees, on the other hand, prioritised political power and social status, disregarding deeper theological and spiritual concerns. The Scribes tended to prioritise legalistic interpretations over the genuine needs and spiritual growth of the people.

WRONG ATTITUDES CAN LEAD US DOWN WRONG PATHS

Instead of embracing the opportunity to learn from Jesus and draw closer to God, the religious leaders of Jesus' day consistently found fault with Him and criticised His actions. They missed the essence of His teachings and the message of love, grace, and salvation that He brought. Their pursuit of applause and recognition from men hindered them from seeking acceptance from God. This wrong attitude of pride and superiority made them enemies of Jesus and His teachings and, sadly, they remained stubborn in their ways, rejecting the truth preached and practiced by Christ right up until His death on the Cross.

Not only did the attitude of the religious leaders lead to their own demise, it also had a negative influence on the people they were meant to be leading. They were always looking for ways to turn the people against Jesus (Matthew 12:22-24). The Jewish people themselves were in need of repentance, yet the majority chose to remain spiritually blind, intensifying their opposition towards Jesus. In observing the hardness of people's hearts, Jesus experienced both anger and grief. He saw the root of bitterness and felt compassion for those at the mercy of the religious leaders. Eventually, Jesus uttered heartfelt words out of deep sorrow and lamentation for Jerusalem, saying: "Jerusalem, Jerusalem, you who kill the prophets and stone those sent to you, how often I have longed to gather your children together, as a hen gathers her chicks under her wings, and you were not willing" (Matthew 23:37). He expressed his heartfelt desire to gather the people of Jerusalem, symbolised by their children, under His loving and protective care, just as a hen gathers her chicks under her wings. However, He recognised their unwillingness to accept Him as their Saviour and their history of rejecting and mistreating the prophets sent by God, leading to His sorrowful plea. Although it is not God's will for anyone to perish, individuals are given the freedom to make choices.

The hatred of the religious leaders towards Jesus reached its boiling point and was openly displayed when they stirred up a mob and seized Him in the Garden of Gethsemane. In fact, even after Jesus was laid in the tomb, the Pharisees went to Pilate, requesting that the tomb be secured to prevent any possibility of the body being stolen (Matthew 27:62-64). After Jesus' resurrection and ascension, the high priest and members of the Sadducee party were filled with jealousy and arrested the apostles (Acts 5:17-18). However, an angel of the Lord freed the apostles from jail, demonstrating God's power over human opposition.

There are several verses of Scripture where Jesus makes it clear that this wrong attitude of the religious leaders would lead them down the wrong path (see Matthew 21:31-32; Luke 18:9-14; Matthew 9:10-13 and Luke 15:1-7, for example). Jesus often challenged the religious leaders by pointing out the stark contrast between their outward righteousness and their inward condition. He taught that true righteousness was not merely about observing religious rituals and following the letter of the law but also about having a genuine heart for God. Jesus boldly proclaimed that prostitutes, tax collectors, and other sinners who recognised their need for God's forgiveness and turned to Him would enter the kingdom of God ahead of the self-righteous religious leaders. He highlighted that it was not external appearances or religious status that determined one's place in God's kingdom, but rather a humble and repentant heart. Jesus' message shook the religious establishment and challenged their understanding of righteousness and salvation, emphasising the need for a deep transformation of the heart rather than outward compliance with religious norms and traditions.

Similarly, today, there are many leaders who claim to follow Jesus but do not live according to His holy standards. They prioritise their position over loyalty to God, just like the Pharisees and other teachers of the law. The world today is plagued by the consequences of these wrong attitudes, as people stubbornly refuse to practice the art of give and take. Many adopt a self-centred mindset, prioritising their own interests above all else. This prevailing confusion persists because individuals are unwilling to change their attitudes.

It is of utmost importance to be deeply concerned about our personal attitudes. We cannot underestimate the impact our attitudes have on our actions, relationships, and overall well-being. Just like the Pharisees, who should have recognised their own repugnant behaviour, we must understand the significance of our attitudes. Our lives should revolve around fostering healthy relationships within families, resolving conflicts between individuals, and promoting harmony between employers and employees.

To truly magnify God, we must enlarge our thoughts about Him. When faced with overwhelming circumstances, it is essential to speak words that declare God's greatness and power over the situation. We must acknowledge that God is eternal, beyond our human comprehension. No army can defeat Him, and no scholar or Pharisee can confuse His teachings. God is the epitome of power, unchanging, and He stands as our Redeemer, Saviour, Lord, and Guide.

Oftentimes, people know that their attitudes are wrong, but they refuse the change. The Pharisees, of all people, should have put away their bad attitudes and recognised Jesus as the chosen One sent from God—the Messiah. After all, they had the Scriptures and knew them well. However, they refused to acknowledge Him, as they were unwilling to give up their treasured positions and power. Jesus exposed their attitude and became their enemy instead of their Messiah.

A DIFFERENT KIND OF RIGHTEOUSNESS

Gvien what we have learned about the religious leaders, it is no wonder that Jesus warned His disciples and the crowds not to follow the hypocritical examples of the Scribes, Sadducees and Pharisees. These leaders did not practice what they preached and burdened people with heavy loads without offering assistance (Matthew 23:1-4). Their lack of example-worthy behaviour undermined the effectiveness of their teachings. The Pharisees' attitude towards Jesus was driven by jealousy and a desire to protect their own positions and authority. In contrast, Jesus' attitude was rooted in love and a deep concern for the spiritual well-being of the people. He desired to see true repentance and a genuine relationship with God, calling the Pharisees to clean up their lives and fill them with God's principles, leaving no room for Satan to enter (Matthew 23:25-28).

Jesus Christ displayed a righteous anger when confronted with wrongdoing. His anger was not fueled by personal pride or selfish motives, but rather by a zeal for righteousness and justice. Likewise, Jesus teaches us that we need a different kind of righteousness, love, and obedience—a righteousness that surpasses the outward righteousness displayed by the Pharisees. True righteousness comes from what God does within us, not from our own efforts. Our focus should be on God, not on seeking the approval of others. It is crucial to examine our lives for anything that gives rise to wrong attitudes and take necessary action to correct it (Romans 12:2). Finally, it is important to note that anger itself is not inherently wrong; its appropriateness lies in how we channel and direct it.

While the Pharisees were meticulous in their observance of the Law, their hearts remained unchanged even as they appeared to adhere to the laws. This serves as a cautionary reminder for us as well. It is not enough to merely follow religious rituals or external practices; we must allow God to work within us, shaping and renewing our attitudes and inner being (Romans 12:2).

As followers of Christ, we are called to go beyond outward appearances and prioritise the transformation of our hearts and minds. Jesus's teachings challenge us to examine our own lives, identifying any areas where our attitudes may not align with God's principles. Through the power of the Holy Spirit, we can surrender our old ways of thinking and allow God to shape us into individuals who reflect His love, compassion, and righteousness.

The book of Moses clearly speaks of the Israelites responding to care for the poor, mirroring God's love and concern. Jesus told the rich to stop charging interest on loans to needy brothers. God never intended people to profit from other people's misfortune. In contrast to the values of this world, God expects us to care for one another, which is more important than personal gain. Those who give to the poor will not lack, but those who ignore their needs will face curses (see Proverbs 28:27).

Jesus is saying that His listeners need a different kind of righteousness, a more genuine version of the Pharisees' righteousness. Our righteousness comes from what God does in us, not from what we can do on our own. We should be God-centred, not self-centred. Our righteousness must be based on reverence for God, not seeking approval from people. We should examine our lives for anything that causes wrong attitudes and take necessary action to correct it (Matthew 27:62-64).

When faced with the needs of others, our attitudes should reflect acceptance and compassion, as exemplified in the story of the good Samaritan (Luke 10:30-37). It is important for us to understand and learn from different attitudes, just as Jesus used various examples to teach His disciples about loving their neighbours, such as the contrasting attitudes towards the wounded man in the parable of the Samaritan.

Jesus came to reveal God the Father and bring His teachings down to earth. Through His parables, teachings, and life, Jesus explained God's love and principles in a way that people could understand (Matthew 13:34-35). By examining Jesus' actions, principles, and attitudes, we can gain a clearer understanding of God and magnify Him in our thoughts (John 14:9).

Remember, our attitudes should reflect acceptance, compassion, and a willingness to learn from different examples. We should prioritise honouring others over personal accomplishments, seek to understand God more clearly through Jesus' teachings and actions, and be wary of self-centred attitudes like those displayed by the Pharisees and Sadducees. By examining Jesus' life and teachings, we can strive to align our attitudes with His principles and demonstrate love and compassion towards others.

Fifteen

Attitudes Towards Church Leaders

Having a right attitude includes honouring and respecting your leaders, recognising that while your ultimate allegiance is to Christ, you are called to serve Him by supporting and uplifting those in leadership positions. It is important to remember that God does not judge you based on your status or position, but rather looks at the attitude of your heart (1 Samuel 16:7).

Leaders should be supported in their vision with boldness and confidence, knowing that they are not alone in their endeavours. They rely on the prayers, encouragement, and support of those they lead to strengthen themselves and fulfill their calling as servant leaders. Spiritual leaders, in particular, hold onto the Word of God and remind themselves and others not to be troubled or afraid. They understand that the One who lives in them is greater than any challenge or difficulty they may face in the world (John 16:33).

Christian leaders are called, commissioned, and given the assignment of sharing the gospel of Jesus Christ. This assignment involves going and telling sinners about the gospel of salvation and calling them to repentance. They are also responsible for encouraging the weary, comforting those who mourn, and providing comfort in times of loss.

Therefore, as followers of Christ, it is crucial to come alongside our leaders, offering them our prayers, encouragement, and support. By doing so, we contribute to the unity and growth of the body of Christ, allowing leaders to fulfill their God-given role with confidence and effectiveness (1 Thessalonians 5:11).

Believers are expected to show respect to those who have worked hard among them and have authority over them in the Lord. Admonish and hold them in the highest regard in love because of their work (1 Thessalonians 5:12-13). This includes pastors, elders, deacons, and teachers, and also extends to one another in the Lord (Ephesians 4:11-12, Romans 12:10). Express your appreciation and let them know how their leadership has helped you. Thank them for their ministry in your life and remember that they need your support and love. If you say nothing, they will not know what you are thinking (1 Timothy 5:17).

At the same time, it is important not to feel intimidated by people due to status. Instead, recognise that all people are equal in the sight of Christ (Galatians 3:28). While it is natural for people to pay attention to outward appearance and look their best, it is more important to seek and develop inner character. Everyone can see your face, but only God knows your heart. God judges the hearts and true allegiance to Him, along with deeds, not the words we speak. Therefore, our righteousness must surpass that of the religious leaders we examined in the previous chapter. The requirements set by those who consider themselves important based on their position hold no weight. God is not impressed by the positions people hold or by external distinctions. Jesus gave His disciples authority over heaven and earth and commanded them to make disciples, preach, baptise, and teach. This same authority is still valid among all followers today (Matthew 28:18-20).

SOMETIMES LEADERS FALTER

This brings us to the point that sometimes our leaders falter. They are not perfect. Many so-called leaders, like the Pharisees, are known for their knowledge of the Bible but fail to live in accordance with its teachings. They claim to follow Jesus but do not live by His holy standards. This is usually due to underlying wrong motives. When the desire for a position of leadership becomes stronger than loyalty to God, the situation becomes dangerous, as happened with the Pharisees and teachers of the law (Matthew 23:3, Matthew 23:13-15).

This is why the choice in selecting leaders must be made with prayer, fasting and the guidance of the Holy Spirit. We must not do this by outward appearance or favouritism. Just as Samuel was warned not to judge based on appearance alone when choosing Israel's next king, we should not overlook the qualities of individuals who may not possess certain physical or social qualities that society admires. God's judgment is based on faith and character, as only He can see the heart and judge correctly.

God does not rate individuals according to status; He looks at the attitude of the heart.

Church leaders should consistently exercise patience and faithfulness towards their supporters. They should serve the Lord with gladness and set the right example for other believers. The role of leaders is to encourage their followers to become leaders of the gospel themselves (2 Timothy 2:2). Remember that God began a good work in you and is able to complete it (Philippians 1:6). He promised never to leave or forsake you, just as He was with Joshua, Moses, and the prophets (Deuteronomy 31:6, Joshua 1:5). He has therefore given you leaders to guide you and help you to grow so that you can live out the plans He has for your life.

PRAYING FOR YOUR LEADERS

Leadership is not an easy task. Leaders often find themselves at the forefront, bearing the brunt of challenges and attacks. That's why they need our unwavering support and encouragement. We must be positive friends who stand with them, celebrating their successes and offering a helping hand in times of need.

Prayer is a powerful tool in upholding our leaders. Regularly lifting them up in prayer, we seek God's wisdom, guidance, and strength to be poured out upon them. Our prayers become a source of strength and fortitude for their journey as servant leaders.

It is also essential to avoid every kind of negativity that could hinder the unity and growth of the body of Christ. Speaking evil of our leaders or about one another goes against the principles of honour and respect the Bible teaches. Instead, we should practice discretion, obedience, and engage in sensible discussions that sharpen our perspectives.

In all things, let us commend ourselves to patience, tribulations, distress, and strive to honour our leaders in love. Let us offer our prayers, encouragement, and support, knowing that by doing so, we contribute to the unity and growth of the body of Christ. Through our honour and respect, leaders are strengthened to fulfill their God-given role with confidence and effectiveness.

Here are some useful Scripture references to meditate on:

Hebrews 13:17: "Have confidence in your leaders and submit to their authority because they keep watch over you as those who must give an account."

1 Timothy 2:1-2: "I urge, then, first of all, that petitions, prayers, intercession, and thanksgiving be made for all people— for kings and all those in authority, that we may live peaceful and quiet lives in all godliness and holiness."

Matthew 20:26-28: "Instead, whoever wants to become great among you must be your servant, and whoever wants to be first must be your slave— just as the Son of Man did not come to be served, but to serve, and to give his life as a ransom for many."

Sixteen

Attitudes Towards Money, Wealth And Service

The love of money is not inherently evil, as money can be used for good purposes. Money is used to purchase properties, provide for the necessities of life such as food, support charities, pay taxes, repair God's house, provide for the poor and needy, and support missionaries. However, it becomes dangerous when we develop the wrong attitude and selfishly prioritise it, deceiving ourselves with a false sense of security and power. Just as the wealth of the Israelites could not save them from Babylon's invasion, our riches will be worthless at the final judgement. What truly matters for eternity is Christ's redemptive work on our behalf.

God is the giver of money; He blesses His people with silver and gold because He does not need them. Instead of expressing gratitude for God's gifts, some people misuse silver and gold by fashioning idols and worshipping them as gods. In reality, these resources should be used for fruitful endeavours and to fulfill God's will.

It is tragic that many people spend so much time and energy pursuing more money to satisfy themselves, while neglecting the pursuit of God, who is the ultimate source of true satisfaction. The love of money poses a serious problem for so many. It is often misused to fulfill selfish desires, abusing God's gifts and diverting resources from their intended purpose. Despite the overwhelming evidence to the contrary, many still hold the belief that money brings happiness. To the contrary, humanity is guilty of allowing the love of money to lead them into sin, not happiness.

This is why the Word of God sternly warns against the love of money, which can become an idol in this world. It possesses a strange power that entices people into sin. As said, it is not sinful to possess money, but when the love of money takes precedence in our hearts and becomes an idol, it leads us astray. This is evident in society, governments, leadership, families, and even within the church. Many are ensnared by the notion that money can solve every problem. They throw money at their issues, seeking the temporary thrill of winning, but soon find that the satisfaction fades, leaving them with the need to acquire even more.

Gratitude is the antidote to the love of money. When we cultivate a grateful heart, we acknowledge that money is a gift from God, meant to be used wisely and in alignment with His purposes. Gratitude reminds us that true contentment and fulfillment come from a relationship with God, not from material possessions. It shifts our focus from accumulation to generosity, from self-centredness to worship, and from relying on money to relying on God's provision.

We must guard our hearts against the love of money and instead embrace gratitude as a guiding principle. May we use the resources God has entrusted to us for His glory, seeking first His kingdom and righteousness. In doing so, we will discover the true richness and abundant life found in honouring God with our finances and aligning our priorities with His eternal purposes.

A wise person will take into consideration that life was designed for companionship, relationships, fellowship, friendship, and both isolation and being on your own. It stresses spiritual prosperity over material prosperity. Thus, the apostle wrote, "For we brought nothing into the world, and we can take nothing out of it. But if we have food and clothing, we will be content with that" (1 Timothy 6:7). Scripture does not portray material poverty as a virtue in itself, but it warns of the temptation of theft that extreme poverty may bring. For example, people may fall into poverty due to their own fault, spending what they don't have, becoming lazy, and refusing to work, becoming a burden to others in society, not reminding themselves of the rule, "If a man does not work, he shall not eat" (see 2 Thessalonians 3:10).

THE RICH YOUNG MAN'S DILEMMA

A significant encounter occurred when a rich young man approached Jesus, humbly kneeling before Him, seeking guidance on inheriting eternal life (see Matthew 19:16-30). Jesus, perceiving the heart of the young man, responded by challenging his attachment to earthly wealth. He instructed him to sell all his possessions and distribute the proceeds to the poor. This command was intended to reveal the young man's true priorities and test his willingness to surrender his material wealth for the sake of the Kingdom.

Sadly, the young man was unable to part with his riches. His love for money outweighed his desire for eternal life. Overwhelmed by sorrow, he walked away, choosing to hold tightly to his possessions rather than embracing the call to follow Jesus wholeheartedly.

The story of the rich young man serves as a poignant reminder of the crucial role our attitude towards money and possessions plays in our spiritual journey. When we prioritise wealth above all else, it becomes a stumbling block in our relationship with God. The love of money has the potential to blind us to the needs of others, inhibiting our capacity to love and serve God wholeheartedly.

Throughout the Bible, we are repeatedly cautioned about the transient nature of wealth. Proverbs 23:5 warns us not to fixate on riches, as they possess the ability to vanish unexpectedly, like an eagle soaring into the sky. Our relentless pursuit of money and material possessions can consume us, leaving us disenchanted and unfulfilled.

It is vital to maintain a balanced perspective, recognising that material wealth, though not inherently evil, can easily distract us from what truly matters—our relationship with God and the well-being of our fellow human beings. Instead of allowing the pursuit of wealth to consume us, we should adopt an attitude of gratitude, contentment, and generosity.

Gratitude reminds us of God's provision and cultivates a spirit of thankfulness for the blessings we have received. Contentment allows us to find joy and fulfillment in God's presence, rather than constantly seeking satisfaction in material possessions. Generosity flows from a heart that recognises the temporal nature of wealth and invests in eternal treasures by serving others and supporting God's kingdom work.

The story of the rich young man serves as a cautionary tale, inviting us to reflect on our own priorities and attitudes towards money and possessions. Let us not allow the love of money to hinder our pursuit of God and impede our ability to love and serve others. Instead, may we approach wealth with wisdom, gratitude, contentment, and a generous heart, recognising that our true wealth lies in our relationship with God and our eternal inheritance.

CORRELATION BETWEEN MONEY AND SERVICE

There is a close correlation between our attitude towards money and our commitment to serving God and others. Instead of prioritising the pursuit of wealth, the Scriptures encourage us to seek first the kingdom of God and His righteousness (Matthew 6:33). This implies being good stewards of the resources entrusted to us, using them wisely and generously. When our hearts are aligned with God's purposes, we can find true contentment and joy, regardless of our financial circumstances.

The Bible repeatedly emphasises the importance of giving to those in need. In 1 Timothy 6:18, we are instructed "to be rich in good deeds, and to be generous and willing to share". By demonstrating generosity and a willingness to help others, we reflect God's character and showcase our love for Him.

However, the love of money extends beyond mere financial considerations. It is a spiritual issue, intertwined with matters of the heart and our priorities. While money can serve as a useful tool when aligned with God's principles, it becomes a stumbling block when it takes precedence over our relationship with God and our love for others.

True generosity goes beyond monetary gifts alone. It encompasses various forms of giving, such as dedicating our time and offering homemade gifts that cost little financially but are brimming with love. The growth in our new life is evident in our attitude towards giving. A key principle is to give cheerfully, not based on the amount given, but on a cheerful heart, a spirit of generosity, and the recognition that what remains after giving is what truly matters. God is more concerned with our motive behind giving than the quantity of the gift. Everything in the world belongs to God, so our gifts to Him do not make us spiritually richer. Rather, our acknowledgement of everything we possess and the amount we give becomes a way to express our love for God.

The Apostle Paul provided guidance to the early church on giving, emphasising regularity and systematicity. In 1 Corinthians 16:2, he instructed each person to set something aside on the first day of the week, giving proportionately as they prospered.

Consider the cautionary tale of a certain king who received abundant prosperity and power from God. Nebuchadnezzar, the king of Babylon, as recorded in the book of Daniel, was a powerful and prosperous king, but his arrogance and pride led to God humbling him by taking away his sanity for a period of time. It served as a lesson about the consequences of misusing the blessings and power granted by God and the importance of humility and acknowledging God's sovereignty. God detests the sin of pride, and when we become forgetful, ungrateful, and develop a wrong attitude, it paves the way for pride to take root.

It is natural to feel elation when achieving significant accomplishments. However, it is crucial not to be disdainful towards God or look down on others. Instead, evaluate your attitude, giving credit to God for what you possess and using your gifts with gratitude and care. True joy comes when you willingly give from the heart, without grudges or seeking attention. Let the words we speak and the actions we take flow from a genuine heart because empty gestures and murmurs of gratitude hold no value. Instead, show kindness and generosity to others, exemplifying the love of Christ. Even if you are financially blessed, when the opportunity arises to give as the Lord prospers, consider whether you would be willing to give for a worthy cause, imagining yourself in the same position of need.

Let us remember that our perspective on money and possessions profoundly impacts our relationship with God and our ability to serve others. Seek God's kingdom first, be generous in good works, and approach giving with a grateful and sincere heart. By doing so, we align ourselves with God's purposes and reflect His love in the world.

THE BEST GIFT: OFFERING YOURSELF AS A LIVING SACRIFICE

The most valuable gift we can offer to the Lord is not material possessions but ourselves. Romans 12:1 reminds us to present our bodies as living sacrifices, holy and pleasing to God. This sacrificial offering does not require physical death but rather a willingness to give from what we have, even if it involves sacrifice and discomfort.

In the Old Testament, animal sacrifices symbolised the need for atonement and forgiveness of sins. However, the death of Jesus on the cross fulfilled and surpassed those sacrifices. As God's only begotten Son, Jesus became the ultimate living sacrifice. In response to His sacrifice, Christ calls all His followers to lay aside their own desires, follow Him wholeheartedly, and dedicate their energy and resources to His service. This act of giving is rooted in gratitude for the forgiveness of our sins.

Jesus taught about the motives behind our giving to God. He advised us not to let our left hand know what our right hand is doing when giving to the needy, emphasising the importance of secret and selfless giving (Matthew 6:3-4). It is easy for our hearts to be willing to give, but our flesh might resist. Therefore, aligning our actions with the intentions of our hearts is crucial.

We must examine our motives in giving to God. It is common to give with mixed motives, expecting something in return or seeking personal gain. However, our giving should be driven by love, gratitude, and a response to God's love for us. The amount we give is not as important as the heart behind our giving. God is concerned with the resources we have and how we cultivate and use them for His purposes.

By sowing seeds in various fields, we can reap an abundant harvest to help those in need. Let respect and humility characterise our attitude towards the well-being of others. Giving ourselves away, allowing God to use us for His kingdom, is the ultimate and most meaningful gift we can offer.

Sometimes, it may be easier to give when others are watching or when we seek recognition. However, we should ensure that our giving flows from a genuine heart of love and gratitude, not from selfish motives. Jesus encourages us to examine our motives in three areas: giving our time generously through acts like fasting and prayer, doing so with a God-centred focus rather than seeking personal praise, and avoiding self-centred acts that negate the spirit of sacrifice.

GIVING TO ALLEVIATE POVERTY

"He who is kind to the poor lends to the Lord and will be rewarded" (Proverbs 19:17). Helping the poor honours both the Creator and His creation. God accepts acts of kindness towards the poor as if they were offered directly to Him. God loves all His creation, regardless of their wealth or poverty. Those who have never experienced poverty may struggle to understand its hardships and challenges. Blaming the poor for their circumstances overlooks the systemic factors that contribute to poverty. While wise planning, ambitious actions, and determination can help individuals improve their situation, being born into privilege or poverty is not within our control.

Jesus acknowledged that poverty would always be present among humanity, stating to His disciples, *"For you will always have the poor with you, and whenever you want, you can do* good for them. But you will not always have me" (Mark 14:7). This recognition does not imply indifference or inhumane treatment towards the poor. On the contrary, Jesus taught us to show compassion, encouragement, and practical help to those in need, working towards positive change in their lives. It is important to differentiate between those facing genuine hardship and those who may exhibit idleness or rebellion, but we should not let these distinctions prevent us from extending a helping hand.

In one instance, Jesus observed a widow in the temple area known as the "court of women". She gave all she had to live on, while the rich individuals present made contributions out of their abundance (Mark 12:41-44). Jesus commended the widow's sacrificial giving and highlighted the value of generosity that goes beyond convenience. As believers, we are called to consider giving, whether it is financial resources, time, or talents, in a way that reflects sacrificial love and compassion. God desires to open our eyes to the needs of the poor and marginalised, urging us not to ignore their plight but to actively contribute to their well-being. In doing so, we will experience God's blessings.

The issue of poverty has persisted throughout history, with the number of poor individuals often exceeding those who possess an abundance of material wealth. Jesus acknowledged the reality of human imperfection and the tendency for pretentious acts related to poverty. He emphasised the importance of compassionately caring for the poor, saying, "Whenever you want, you can do good for them" (Mark 14:7). The Bible presents a balanced perspective, expressing empathy for those suffering from severe oppression while admonishing those who harm themselves through unwise choices.

As Christian believers, we are taught the significance of supporting God's work and the well-being of others. The Scriptures also encourage personal responsibility and the importance of work. The Apostle Paul wrote, *"If anyone is not willing to work, let him not eat"* (2 Thessalonians 3:10). Those who are physically able should be willing to work and take responsibility for themselves and their families, rather than relying on others for their sustenance. The example of the ant is cited in Proverbs 6:6-11, highlighting their diligence and ability to gather provisions. We are called to use our energy and resources wisely, planning for the future and fulfilling our responsibilities.

While acknowledging the existence of poverty, we are called to respond with compassion, practical assistance, and sacrificial giving. We should not overlook the needs of the poor but actively seek ways to make a positive impact in their lives. At the same time, personal responsibility and diligence are emphasised, encouraging individuals to work and provide for themselves and their families. By embracing these principles, we demonstrate the love and care that Jesus taught us and participate in bringing about positive change in the world.

HOW SHOULD WE VIEW MENIAL TASKS?

Having a positive attitude towards menial tasks is a valuable quality that can greatly impact one's character and reputation. There is a story of an admirable young woman, found in the Old Testament book of Ruth, that exemplifies this attitude, as she displayed qualities such as love, kindness, bravery, and a strong work ethic. While the focus of the story lies in the faithfulness and redemption experienced by two individuals, we can also draw valuable lessons about the significance of embracing humility and performing even seemingly insignificant tasks with diligence and love.

Naomi, a widow who had endured immense loss, returned to Bethlehem accompanied by her devoted daughter-in-law, Ruth. Their arrival caused a stir in the community, with people wondering why Naomi had returned empty-handed. However, Ruth's unwavering loyalty and determination shone through her willingness to undertake menial tasks to sustain herself and Naomi.

Embracing the concept of gleaning, Ruth humbly ventured into the fields to gather leftover grain, ensuring their survival. This act, though seemingly mundane, displayed her dedication and selflessness. It serves as a powerful reminder that positive tasks, such as caring for the sick, supporting family members, or engaging in acts of service, even if they appear menial, hold great value.

As Ruth gleaned in the fields, she found herself in the portion belonging to Boaz, a relative of Naomi's late husband. Boaz noticed Ruth's diligence and her heart of service, and he extended kindness towards her, instructing his workers to leave extra grain for her to collect. This act of generosity not only provided for Ruth and Naomi's immediate needs but also showcased the impact of a good attitude towards tasks that may seem insignificant.

Inspired by Naomi's wisdom and guided by her counsel, Ruth eventually found herself at the threshing floor where Boaz was spending the night. In an act of humility and seeking Boaz's protection as a kinsman-redeemer, she lay at his feet. While this encounter holds deeper significance within the biblical narrative, it also exemplifies Ruth's willingness to embrace tasks that others might deem beneath them, showcasing her commitment to a higher purpose.

The story of Naomi, Ruth, and Boaz, told here to emphasise the importance of a positive attitude towards seemingly menial tasks, serves as a powerful reminder that true worth is not measured by the nature of the task itself but by the spirit in which it is carried out. By acknowledging the value of tasks such as sitting with the sick, preparing meals, or engaging in acts of service, we can embody the humility, love, and dedication demonstrated by Ruth and find fulfillment in serving others. Ultimately, it is through these seemingly insignificant tasks that we can make a lasting impact on the lives of those around us and experience the blessings of God's providence.

LAZY ATTITUDES

God does not oppose human effort and the diligent pursuit of a just cause that honours Him. However, when work becomes a means to exclude or neglect one's family, it may indicate a lack of trust in God's provision. It is essential to have a proper understanding of the genuine needs of others. Rest and spiritual refreshment are necessary, but they should never be excuses for laziness. Sadly, we often encounter individuals who are labeled as lazy or workaholics.

The lazy person folds their hands and idly watches others toil for an honest living. On the other hand, the workaholic is driven by envy and greed, constantly striving to outpace everyone else. Both extremes are foolish and should be avoided. We must distinguish between leisure, laziness, relaxation, and recreation, as they bring necessary balance to our lives. Lazy individuals should be willing to use their time and talents to provide for themselves. Independence plays a vital role in personal well-being, though the church should always offer support to individuals and families in need. Let us not forget to show our support and appreciation for church leaders who guide and serve us.

Congregational leaders should actively encourage believers to seek gainful employment and discourage idleness. Implementing projects and initiatives that engage everyone in productive work, fostering independence, can be of great help. Sometimes individuals may exhibit a lazy attitude, while others may be shy or fearful of making mistakes. In ministry, it is important to approach these situations with sensitivity, carefully assessing the underlying issues and providing appropriate remedies to shift their mindset away from passivity.

It is crucial to heed Solomon's warning found in the book of Proverbs regarding laziness. When morning comes, resisting the temptation to give in to laziness and instead embracing the call to work is crucial. Rest is vital, but surrendering to the allure of laziness and completely avoiding work is wrong. God designated the Sabbath as a day of rest and restoration, and there is a time for everything under the sun. We can gain valuable lessons from the example of the ant, which diligently uses its energy and resources.

Solomon's wisdom cautions against laziness and the potential consequences of poverty. Those who sleep during the harvest, wasting their time pursuing empty fantasies and resources, will find themselves desiring abundance but receiving very little. Laziness leads to a state of real poverty and ongoing troubles. Neglecting to sow and plow the field, while making hasty excuses for one's circumstances, will result in genuine poverty caused by laziness. Let us be mindful of these admonitions and strive for diligence and responsibility in our lives.

BE CONSISTENT IN YOUR ATTITUDE

An attitude of consistency is of utmost importance when it comes to reaping great rewards and staying committed until the end. In our walk with God, it is crucial to maintain consistency in prayer, supplication, and thanksgiving, as this brings fulfillment and abundant rewards. With God's help, we can navigate life's journey safely and reach the ultimate finish line.

The Scriptures encourage us to persevere in constant prayer. It should be a consistent practice, a lifestyle rather than a sporadic event. Just as engaging in righteous activities consistently forms a positive habit that becomes deeply ingrained, consistently indulging in evil forms a destructive pattern. We cannot serve both righteousness and wickedness simultaneously. We must choose to be consistent in doing good, forsaking the allure of wrong paths. Regarding this, Jesus Himself has words of wisdom to offer.

Jesus once denounced those who honoured Him with their lips but had hearts far from Him. He confronted the hypocrisy of those who claimed to worship God but their actions were insincere. Good intentions alone are insufficient if our deeds and motives lack authenticity. It is essential to regularly examine our attitudes towards God and our fellow human beings. Jesus described the behaviour of hypocrites who approached God as mere actors, professional worshippers who prayed in public but lacked genuine love in their hearts. They stood apart from others, making a show of their devotion through empty words and superficial displays of affection. However, their hearts were distant from God, habitually estranged and alienated.

Such behaviour can breed bitterness, control our emotions, prolong pain, and damage relationships. It can lead to a sour disposition and a tendency to gossip about the actions and words of others. The way we perceive and treat others often reflects our own attitude. The only true solution is forgiveness and turning to God, who sees all things and is a God of justice. By adopting the right attitude and forgiving one another, we open ourselves to the forgiveness of our Heavenly Father. Conversely, if we withhold forgiveness from others, our Heavenly Father will also withhold forgiveness from us.

Maintaining a negative attitude towards someone we are praying for is indeed challenging. Jesus instructed His followers to love their enemies, even though many failed to grasp the depth of His teaching and turned away. Loving our enemies does not imply having affection for them, but rather making a deliberate choice to act in their best interest and think of ways to help them. Jesus loved the entire world, even though the world rebelled against God. His message to us is to pray for those who mistreat us and find ways to reach out to them, embracing the nine fruits of the Spirit as our approach: love, joy, peace, patience, kindness, goodness, faithfulness, gentleness, and self-control. As Christians, we should approach God with reverence, bowing our heads low yet unafraid to make our requests known. Some may pray flippantly, giving little thought to their petitions or failing to approach God with the respect He deserves. God is our King, and He invites us to come to Him with boldness and assurance, as friends.

The secret to consistency lies in wholeheartedly trusting that God never changes and remains unshaken by the fluctuations of the world. He endures forever, and no worldly ideas can alter His unchanging nature. "Those who trust in the Lord are like Mount Zion, which cannot be shaken but endures forever" (Psalm 125:1). Consistency in our faith means having the unwavering ability to trust in God regardless of circumstances. It means believing in the fulfillment of His promises even when we cannot see the outcome, treating it as already accomplished or in progress. Envisioning faith is a positive practice, and genuine faith produces consistent character. Those who are easily swayed by every wind and influenced by various ideas are inconsistent and unreliable.

Consistency should be a hallmark of believers, as even a gradual deviation from God for a brief moment can lead to spiritual coldness and minor departures from His commandments. A small sin can grow and ultimately lead to downfall. We should not allow unknown or excused sins to go unchallenged in our lives. Living for God requires consistent spirituality in all areas, with a fully surrendered attitude that acknowledges Him. We must guard our desires, seeking to align them with Jesus, and endeavour to keep all aspects of our lives within the boundaries of God's will and in our relationships. It is essential to be cautious and avoid associating with bad company, engaging in wrongful actions, and allowing unaddressed sin to take root.

A negative and wrong attitude can spread like a deadly cancer, slowly eroding joy and relationships with God and others. Therefore, it is important to confess known faults and failures to God, seeking His strength to resist temptation. This confession should occur promptly before these urges become unrecognizable. A family without God will never experience the spiritual bond that God imparts to those in a relationship with Him. Every aspect of life requires God's involvement from the initial planning and preparation. If we desire successful outcomes, why not prioritise God in everything we hope to achieve? (Psalm 127)

Seventeen

Unthankful Attitudes

W hen was the last time you paused to genuinely give thanks from the depths of your heart? Giving thanks is a transformative action that goes beyond mere words; it is an expression of gratitude and appreciation for the countless blessings we have received, both from others and from God Himself. By uttering those two simple words, "thank you," we not only convey our gratitude but also escape the label of being ungrateful.

As humans, we often struggle with a lack of gratitude, both towards one another and towards God. It is far too easy for us to become forgetful creatures, taking things for granted and failing to acknowledge and express thanks to those who have provided for us. We may even find ourselves hesitant to apologise when we are in the wrong, dismissing our actions with empty phrases like "I never meant it that way." Yet, in doing so, we undermine the power of gratitude and the importance of owning up to our mistakes.

It is crucial for us to cultivate a heart of gratitude, even in the midst of waiting for our prayers to be answered. There are times when God's response may seem silent, and His timing may puzzle us. However, we must remember that His silence does not indicate inaction, nor does it imply that He is unconcerned about our circumstances. On the contrary, He is always at work behind the scenes, orchestrating events for our ultimate good, even when we cannot perceive it.

A heart filled with gratitude is indeed a heart that overflows with blessings, as the Bible encourages us to remain grateful. In 1 Thessalonians 5:18, we are reminded to *"Give thanks in all circumstances; for this is the will of God in Christ Jesus for you."* Even when circumstances may not seem favourable, trusting in the power of gratitude allows us to experience its fruitful impact in our lives.

Psalm 136:1 echoes the call to give thanks to the Lord, acknowledging His goodness and enduring love. It serves as a reminder that regardless of how things may appear, God's love remains steadfast and His goodness never wavers.

Furthermore, in the Book of Romans, we find encouragement and assurance that God sees the bigger picture and works all things together for the good of those who love Him and are called according to His purpose. Romans 8:28 reminds us, *"And we know that in all things God works for the good of those who love him, who have been called according to his purpose."*

These verses remind us of the importance of maintaining an attitude of gratitude, even in the face of challenges or uncertainties. By trusting in God's unfailing love, goodness, and His perfect plan, we can find strength, peace, and hope in every circumstance. Let us hold onto these truths and continue to cultivate a heart of gratitude, knowing that God is faithful and His blessings abound.

Therefore, let us embrace a lifestyle of gratitude, expressing thanks for the blessings we have received and acknowledging the goodness of God in our lives. Even in moments of waiting, let us trust in His faithfulness and steadfast love, knowing that He is continually working on our behalf. Gratitude transforms our perspective and fills our hearts with hope and joy, reminding us that God's plans are perfect, and His ways are higher than ours.

The worst attitude one can have is showing ungratefulness towards God, the giver of life, without considering the vastness of His unmerited kindness and favour. Without God, we would not dare to live or die. For instance, God showed grace and kindness to Israel throughout their existence. He loved them and chose them when they were a multiplying nation in Egypt. Even when they were helpless, foolish, outcast, and exposed, God loved them, saying in Hosea 14:4: "*I will heal their waywardness and love them freely, for my anger has turned away from them.*"

God delivered them from bondage, taught them to make right decisions and obey His commandments. He provided them with ceremonial laws as tutors, acted as their physician when anything was wrong, and healed them while they were in Egypt. Jeremiah 3:12 says, "*Return, faithless Israel, declares the LORD. I will not look on you in anger, for I am merciful, declares the LORD; I will not be angry forever.*" And He was not. He fed them with food from heaven and gently brought them into His service. He drew them with cords of love, eased their burdens, and treated them mercifully, like a good husbandman who cares for his animals and does not overwork them. We read in Isaiah 41:17: *"When the poor and needy seek water, and there is none, and their tongue is parched with thirst, I the LORD will answer them; I the God of Israel will not forsake them."*

Unfortunately, the people became unthankful, disobedient, and turned a deaf ear to God's voice. They became fond of worshipping idols instead of showing gratitude to God for His blessings. Idolatry was always a sin that easily beset them. They grew ignorant, which was the root of ingratitude, and hardened their hearts and necks, refusing to repent even when God sent prophets and ministers to warn them. They carved idols out of the same trees that provided them with firewood, idols that profited them nothing. In reality, an idol is anything that is given a sacred value and power. It is sensible to ask, "Who created me? Who do I trust? Where do I find security and happiness? Who is in charge of my future?" All who worship other gods should consider these questions. Therefore, God's judgments would come upon them unless they repented and turned from their foolish ways. God's heart is just, and His mercy would ultimately spare them. Though the people would be corrected, they would not be consumed because God is not a man; He is the Holy One of Israel. If the people seek the face of the Lord, walk in His ways, and have a thankful attitude towards God, He would be willing to accept them as His beloved people.

Let us therefore examine our hearts and ensure that we maintain a posture of gratitude towards God, for His love and mercy are always available to those who seek Him with a thankful spirit.

God's love is unconditional, and He desires that you have no other gods besides Him. It is easy to take God's mercies for granted, but you should remember that it is God who shows mercy, not you. Show gratitude instead of using His mercy without giving thanks. If you do, you will not be consumed. "Great is God's faithfulness." The people who received kindness did not take it to heart and give God thanks for His blessings. Instead, they showed ungratefulness and an inconsiderate attitude towards God. Therefore, take a moment to think about the small mercies you receive on a daily basis and be thankful for these quiet blessings.

THE TRANSFORMATIVE POWER OF GRATITUDE

There was a man named Micah who had a quarrel with his mother because he stole her carefully saved money, 1000 pieces of silver. The old woman had preserved this sum, perhaps with the intention of leaving it to her son in her will, as an act of love and provision. However, Micah's actions displayed a lack of gratitude, as he failed to recognise the value and effort his mother had invested in saving that money for his future.

The mother, understandably hurt and mistrusting, cursed her son for taking her hard-earned money. This highlights how the mischief of money can destroy relationships and create strife when gratitude is absent. Micah soon realised the gravity of his actions and became terrified of his mother's curse. In a moment of repentance and understanding the importance of gratitude, he made the decision to return the stolen money to his mother.

Witnessing Micah's sincere repentance and acknowledging his gratitude, the mother was pleased and revoked the curses she had spoken. She turned her curses into heartfelt prayers for her son's welfare, embracing forgiveness and reconciliation.

This story serves as a powerful illustration of the importance of gratitude. Micah's initial ungratefulness and theft strained his relationship with his mother. However, his act of returning the money demonstrated a profound change of heart and a realisation of the value of gratitude. By expressing his appreciation and making amends, Micah restored the bond with his mother.

Through this narrative, we see that gratitude has the power to heal and restore relationships. It has much in common with repentence. It teaches us to recognise and appreciate the blessings bestowed upon us by others. Micah's transformation showcases how gratitude can mend the damage caused by ungrateful behaviour, leading to reconciliation and fostering a deeper sense of love and appreciation.

In our own lives, this story reminds us of the importance of cultivating gratitude. It prompts us to reflect on the efforts and sacrifices made by others on our behalf. By expressing gratitude, we honour those who have supported and cared for us, and we nurture healthy and harmonious relationships. Ultimately, this story encourages us to embrace gratitude as a transformative virtue that enriches our lives and the lives of those around us.

AFTER THOUGHT

After much reflection and consideration, I bring this remarkable book on the theme of Attitude to a close. I am overwhelmed with gratitude and compelled to thank God for His unwavering help, guidance, and inspiration throughout the process of writing this concluding chapter. From the very first chapter to this final one, I have sought inspiration and insight from various sources, particularly eternal truths. Each chapter has been bathed in prayer and careful consideration for the benefit of my readers. This book holds a special place in my heart as I share personal and transformative experiences, illustrating how I have shifted from negativity to positive thinking in my interactions with others, irrespective of their age or wealth.

My sincere hope is that this book becomes a valuable tool for you to discover your purpose in God. The examples I have presented throughout these pages are drawn from the lives of esteemed men and women who exemplify extraordinary character, showcasing their approach to dealing with challenging behaviours. If you have ever felt overwhelmed by insurmountable odds, take heart, for there is help available. Proceed with confidence, knowing that God is present and the author of all existence. No problem is beyond His ability to solve, and no circumstance is too trivial for His attention. He sees you where you are, and you are securely held in His grasp. "If God is for you, who can be against you?"

Witnessing God's restorative power is truly awe-inspiring. His ability to bring new life even from the ashes of burned forests surpasses our comprehension. Broken bones mend, and grief, though agonising, is not everlasting—it will pass, and your tears can become seeds that will flourish into a bountiful harvest once again.

Maintaining the right attitude and patient anticipation for God's miraculous intervention in any situation can test one's faith. However, I am confident that this book will serve as an inspiration to all readers, just as it has been to me. It has compelled me to make significant and necessary changes in my own attitude.

The process of writing and sharing my story has been an immensely rewarding experience. At times, it felt as if my thoughts and aspirations were ignited by an external force, momentarily pausing before resuming with an even greater release of positive energy for each chapter.

Of course, the treasures to be discovered in the Word of God are inexhaustible, so this book can only represent a fraction of what is available. Remember to take time out to read, pray over and apply the Scriptures for yourself.

Wishing you joy and fulfillment as you continue on the journey of reading and discovery of God's word for your life.

ABOUT THE AUTHOR

Meet Phyllis Jemmott, a devoted Christian writer with a burning passion for spreading the Word of God through her writing. For many years, Phyllis has delved deep into the Scriptures, unearthing precious nuggets of wisdom to share with the world. Her dedication to her craft has led her to publish five remarkable books, each touching the hearts and minds of readers in unique ways.

In 2012, Phyllis released her first book, *A Guide to Effective Prayer*. This powerful work was born out of her own challenging life experiences. Through the exercise of prayer, Phyllis discovered the tools to rise above every obstacle and find solace at the feet of the Master.

The following year, in 2013, Phyllis authored *After the Honeymoon*, a book aimed at inspiring newlywed couples embarking on the voyage of marriage. Drawing from her own insights and experiences, Phyllis provides guidance and encouragement for couples as they navigate the early stages of their marital journey.

In 2021, Phyllis penned *God is Always Right*, a timeless book intended for individuals of all walks of life. With simplicity and clarity, she reminds readers, both young and old, rich and poor, that God's wisdom and righteousness are unfailing, serving as a constant reminder of His unchanging love and guidance.

Born out her study of God's names, Phyllis released *The Effectiveness of the Names of God* in 2022. In this enlightening work, she explores the power, authenticity, and ownership associated with the various names ascribed to God. While the number of names may be countless, Phyllis thoughtfully highlights a select few to illuminate the divine attributes they embody.

Continuing her literary journey in 2022, Phyllis published *The Edge*, a thought-provoking book addressing the allure of distractions and the potential pitfalls of straying from the right path. Geared towards those standing on the precipice of their circumstances, Phyllis offers practical guidance to help readers regain their focus and navigate life's challenges with clarity and purpose.

Phyllis Jemmott's literary works embody her unwavering dedication to spreading God's message of love, faith, and redemption. Through her dedication as a writer, she continues to touch the lives of readers, guiding them towards a deeper understanding of God's truth and encouraging them to embrace a life aligned with His purpose.

Printed in Great Britain
by Amazon

25764575R00119